The Technique of
WOOD SURFACE DECORATION

INTARSIA TO BOULLEWORK

DAVID HAWKINS

B. T. Batsford Ltd · London

To Lady Elsie Stoddart-Scott
President of the Chippendale Society
With thanks

Diagrams by Elizabeth Rice

Acknowledgements

Acknowledgements and thanks to Frederick
Drewett and Frank Berendt, colleagues of many
years, and to my wife and daughter Sarah for all
their help.

Alexander & Berendt Ltd., London.
Michael Chevis A.B.I.P.P. A.M.P.A., Midhurst,
Sussex.
Raymond Fortt Studios, Kingston, Surrey.

J. Paul Getty Museum, California.
Boston Museum of Fine Art, Massachusetts.
Detroit Institue of Arts, Michigan.
The Chippendale Society, Otley, Yorkshire.
Nostell Priory, Yorkshire.
Royal Tunbridge Wells Museum, Kent.
Victoria & Albert Museum, London.
Stadt Museum, Cologne.
Jeremy Ltd., London.
Jonathan Harris, London.

First published 1986

© David Hawkins 1986

ISBN 0 7134 4501 7
Printed in Great Britain by
Anchor Brendon Ltd,
Tiptree, Essex

for the Publishers,
B. T. Batsford Ltd,
4 Fitzhardinge Street,
London, W1H OAH

Contents

Picture Acknowledgements

Photographs are the author's unless stated here. (Numbers refer to photo numbers in text.) Alexander and Berendt Ltd/Raymond Fortt Studios, 46. Boston Museum of Fine Art/Raymond Fortt Studios, 12, 13, 14, 14, 16, 17./Michael Chevis, 47, 48. Michael Chevis/Author, 20, Chippendale Society/Raymond Fortt Studios, 106, 107, 108. Cologne, Stadt Museum, 1. Detroit, Institute of Arts, 153, Detroit Institute of Arts/Raymond Fortt Studios, 201. Ebenistes of the Eighteenth Century, 23, 35, 61. J. Paul Getty Museum/Raymond Fortt Studios, 51. Nostell Priory, 3. Private Collections 144, 145, 146. Private Collection/Michael Chevis, 99, 100. Private Collection/Raymond Fortt Studios, 41, 49, 53, 65, 161. Royal Tunbridge Wells Museum, 73, 74, 75, 76, 77, 78, 79. Victoria and Albert Museum, 4. World Furniture, 5. Wrightsman Collection, Volume 1, 24.

Colour plate (iv) courtesy Royal Tunbridge Wells Museum.

How it all began: intarsia and veneer

From the beginning man seems to have had the need to express himself in many ways. My purpose is to explore just one. The decoration of dwellings from the earliest cave paintings to the magnificent architecture that we enjoy today has gone hand in hand with the decoration of objects and possessions to go within these architectural triumphs. The decoration of wood has been divided into five methods from the earliest times: painting, gilding, engraving, carving and intarsia. It is intarsia I have selected, since it is from this that the technique of wood surface decoration and the purpose of this book developed.

Intarsia or inlay can safely be called a universal style of decoration. The most costly form is the inlaying of precious stones into solid gold or silver. Exactly the same approach is used when implanting the eyes into a primitive animal carving; the purpose of both techniques is to create a contrast in colour. Intarsia, instead of bringing animation to a carving, can be used to create an object that denotes power, position and wealth.

The use of inlay can be applied to many things. Without the inlays of turquoise, lapis and jet the gold death mask of an Egyptian pharoah would be almost meaningless. A bronze jug is a bronze jug until coloured glass is melted or fired into a surface pattern and the beauty of cloisonné results. A gun or firing-piece is a very ordinary and functional thing, but inlaid with gold, silver, ivory or pearl it will become of such importance and value that it is no longer the weapon of a private soldier, but of a general or king.

Inlaying as a technique can embrace a very

diagram 1

diverse list of materials. This chapter covers just one of these – wood. With wood a vast selection of contrasts and colour is possible. It can produce a simple two-colour pattern as in diagram 1, or a picture that at first glance can appear to be a painting, as in photo 1.

The use of intarsia spread across Europe very swiftly. It may have been transmitted via Portuguese traders: articles brought from the Far East inlaid with ivory, bone and pearl are known as Indo-Portuguese or Goan. Spain's association

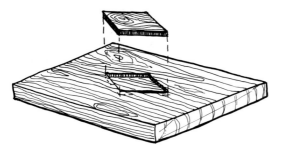

diagram 2

(if that is the word) with the Dutch could certainly have spread the technique to the Netherlands. The capture of a Spanish man-of-war would have enabled Tudor England to see the magnificence of the mahogany and inlay that the great cabins of these galleons are known to have contained.

The best starting place must be to go where the finest results can be seen, fifteenth- and sixteenth-century Italy, and from there to Augsburg, in southern Germany, which became the centre for perhaps the finest exponents of the technique.

The availability of tradesmen with the necessary skills would have been a problem; this was solved by the importation of skills to re-create what had been seen, to meet the increasingly elaborate demands of designers and architects. The names of those working in seventeenth- and eighteenth-century Paris illustrate this; they come from Italy, Germany, the Netherlands and elsewhere. William of Orange brought Daniel Marot to Great Britain, which became a haven of many Huguenot emigrées; the impact of their skills needs no mention here. Many craftsmen migrated to places where work was plentiful and the living better. Their skills became absorbed by their new homelands and played a part in subsequent development.

Inlaying is just what the name implies; the cutting of a shape into solid wood, trenching the shape to an even depth. If the wood is 16mm ($\frac{3}{4}$in) thick we can trench the shape to 4mm ($\frac{3}{16}$in) deep. The shape that has been cut out is then copied in a contrasting colour or grain; this is fixed or glued into place (diagram 2), the two surfaces are made flush or cleaned up and dia-

diagram 3

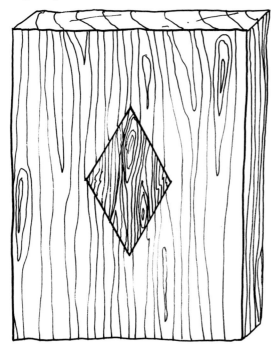

diagram 4

photo 1

photo 2

gram 3 is the result.

Briefly, this is the principle of inlay, and this is the technique most frequently described and illustrated. However, there is a quicker and simpler way. If the solid piece of wood you are to inlay (known as the *ground*) is trenched out to the desired shape first, a pattern must then be transferred from it to the inlay piece, either by drawing, tracing, or taking a rubbing (diagram 4). This process takes time and can lead to error. The easiest and simplest alternative is to make the inlay first, place it in position on the ground, and lightly mark around it with a knife to break the surface fibres. The marked area can now be trenched out to the necessary depth, and ninety-nine times out of a hundred the inlay will fit.

Photo 1 is of a door from a German court cupboard made in Cologne in 1599. To give you an idea of the scale of the decoration, the door is only about 280mm (12in) by 250mm (10in). The

second method described above has been used; the over-running of the marking of the scribing knife to cut around the inlay can be clearly seen. The inlays of the eyes and head-dress create recognition and animation.

A knife is difficult to control; the over-running demonstrates just one minor problem, and this can be seen time and time again with intarsia. Photo 2 shows it again, this time with a honeysuckle of ebony from 1800. The cut is seen at the point. The initial marking cut to break the surface fibres need not be very deep; a method of cutting the ground with good and safe control is needed. This is supplied by a tool called a paying knife (diagram 5). This is very fine and well tempered, held vertically with the point pressed into the initial marking cut. The edge is then tapped with a light hammer along this cut. The knife can be kept firmly under control and complicated shapes can be followed with ease (diagram 6). Over-running is so often found that it can safely be used to define the line between inlay and marquetry.

There is a woodcut from the sixteenth century which depicts a *marqueteur*, the tradesman wearing the traditional cap from those days and using a shoulder knife. This type of knife is similar to the

9

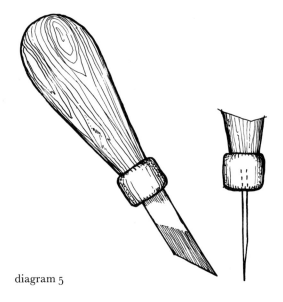

diagram 5

diagram 6

diagram 7

paying knife in the diagram, but the handle is extended to reach from the hand to the shoulder when the upper and lower arm are at 90° to each other. The top of the handle is held on a pad at the shoulder, the left or right hand holding the grip above the blade (diagram 7).

This woodcut assumes the man to be cutting intarsia, which is questionable. With a shoulder knife tremendous pressure and cutting power can be achieved, far more than with the paying knife

and hammer. Furthermore, with a shoulder knife the intricacies of some intarsia must be lost. The woodcut may show the cutting of the near-geometrical patterns of some early inlays, but even this would not require the huge cutting power of a shoulder knife. Perhaps the creation of *pietre dure* or hardstone panels is represented, another form of intarsia from the period. These quite beautiful works with their diversity of stone often carried areas which look exactly like wood – which is what they were before fossilization turned them to stone.

So far the only tools mentioned have been the scribing knife, paying knife, shoulder knife, and hammer. Tools for trenching are also required: chisels, and a flat scratch, set to the inlay depth (diagram 8). This is the fore-runner of the hand router, often called the hag's or nag's tooth, when the simple square scraper of the scratch became the right-angled chisel in this tool (diagram 9). Not very complimentary, but we can see the reason for the nickname. The most important tool of all now comes into the picture, the saw; so

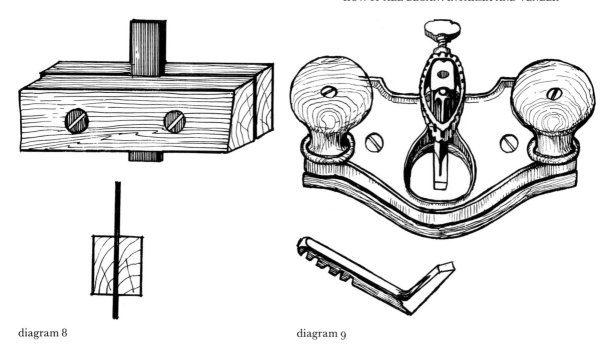

diagram 8   diagram 9

commonplace, yet with more functions, developments and adaptations than any other tool.

Sawing has always been skilled and time consuming. It is skilled enough to carry its own trade of sawyer and saw doctor. The early carpenters used riving or splitting irons to render timbers to some semblance of plank, and this very early preparation is still used today – chestnut paling fence and roof shingle are just two examples. But the saw had to supersede this for the preparation of tree to plank, necessary for stacking and seasoning, and also vital for the initial preparation for panels and carcass wood. More importantly, in a finer form it would prepare the much thinner stocks of contrasting woods for the inlays; and thus the sawyers were preparing the way for the introduction and manufacture of veneer.

Timber, even hardwood, when new, is quite soft and does not require great strength to cut. Few woods were imported during the sixteenth century: the most common was ebony. There are records of some butt-ends of brazil being imported during Tudor times – this we now know was mahogany – but most of the woods used would be indigenous to the country, and even to the area of

manufacture. The list is not large: beech, plane, laburnum, holly, box, chestnut, laurel, hawthorn, lime, almond, walnut, olive, fruitwoods, sycamore, some briars, mulberry, thuya, elm, ash, cedar, oak, brown oak, some pollarded oaks, yew, green oak (caused by fungus), bog yew and bog oak. The two latter do sometimes cause confusion; given more time they would have become the petrified wood of *pietre dure*. Both these woods are just as their name suggests; they have fallen into or in some way become immersed in peat or fen bogs, and their chemistry has reacted with the bog to bring about a change. With yew it is to a very dark brown, whilst oak becomes almost black, which often leads it to be mistaken for ebony. Chemical reactions change the colour and preserve the wood, but never the character and appearance of the wood grain.

At this stage I have only discussed the inlaying of a simple shape of one wood into a solid ground. Each new technique introduced will depend on the previous ones. To explain, look at a two-wood pattern, photo 3. The date is around the first quarter of the seventeenth century and the place of origin England. The ground is oak and the

photo 3

inlays bog oak and holly. The lighter-coloured wood being the holly, you can see that the flowers or decorations on either side are the reverse of each other, like a positive and negative in photography. Again, with the panels in the chest (photo 4), the idea is simple. Take two pieces of wood, one bog oak, the other holly, about 60mm ($2\frac{1}{2}$ in) square and 3mm–4mm ($\frac{1}{8}$ in) thick, and join them together. A fretsaw or coping saw would have been used to cut the panels in photo 4 – probably a coping saw, as the blade appears to have been coarse and fast-cutting. In the sixteenth century the finer fret and piercing saws had not been fully developed. Cut the shape through the two pieces of wood at the one sawing, take them apart, exchange the black and white, and from the one sawing you have the two inlays of diagram 10. When everything is cut out and

photo 4

interchanged, revert to the knife and inlay them into the ground. To prevent the inlays falling apart they can be glued to paper, or – as was used in the early days – vellum, old parchment or coarse cloth.

When you see the magnificence of this work it is hard to believe that these two simple techniques are the basis of it all. Obviously the problems of laying and glueing were huge and had to be got over; how this was achieved will be gone into

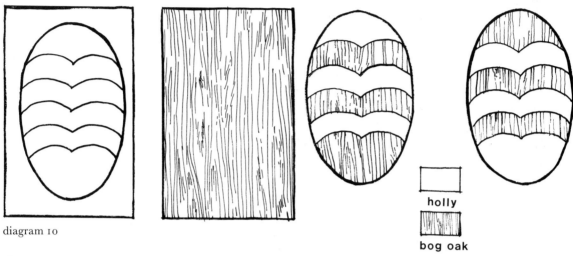

holly

bog oak

diagram 10

photo 5

photo 6

later. The designers raised the efforts of the tradesmen to amazing levels, by the introduction of perspective and the three dimensional effects of photo 5. The lifting handles show that they are the ends of a chest. Other materials – ivory, pearl, tortoiseshell and metals – were often incorporated in these designs. The depth of expression achieved is remarkable. They are even more incredible when you realize that at this time veneer had not yet been introduced.

In the 1980s veneer is taken for granted. Modern technology allows logs to be peeled almost as easily as a pencil is sharpened. Guillotines slice veneers with total accuracy and economy, machines glue it, and the press will lay it at a remarkable speed. Glues can dry almost instantly, and some are totally waterproof.

Veneer seems to be regarded as something that 'just happened', but during the period we have so far been writing about (1500–1620) the only way to produce a veneer was with the saw, and the chances of continuously producing a successful veneer with it would have been (to say the least) small. Because of this early veneers bear no relationship whatsoever to the veneers you see today.

It is important to mention the reasons why veneer was re-introduced. I say 're-introduced' purposely; the ancient Egyptians were certainly able to veneer, and it follows that the Romans and Greeks had mastered it also. Amongst the treasures of Tutankhamun is a box veneered with ebony. This craft seems to have died with the ancient world to re-emerge about 1600–1610, again with the same wood, ebony.

It is said that in the seventeenth century veneers were sawn to about 2mm (about $\frac{1}{8}$ in) in thickness, but my experience suggests that if the veneers are original they needed to carry, when sawn, far more thickness than these measurements allow. Why was veneer used at all? There are three reasons: 1, Economy: 2, it enables rare and exotic wood to go further: 3, it gives the furniture-maker the chance to make a cheap carcass and cover it with a better wood in veneer.

Let us take no. 3 first, mainly because veneer is today often regarded as something inferior and associated with the cheap and cheerful. Nevertheless, you cannot veneer on to a cheap material, and this was probably the reason for the decline in the fortunes of veneer in the mid-nineteenth century. With the introduction of huge circular saws, it became too easy to produce: photo 6 shows the sawing kerfs of a nineteenth-century veneer. This mechanization produced veneers of such finish that preparation or toothing of them was often not carried out, or necessary. Time and again veneers from these dates, when removed, have demonstrated this point. This development allowed veneers and their preparation and laying to become progressively cheaper with the result that much shoddy work was produced. The finest is not remembered, the cheap and cheerful is. A lack of respect for veneer is illustrated by Dickens, in the *Pickwick Papers*, chapter XIV. In 'The bagman story' the old chair moans, 'Dammee you would not treat me with less respect if I was veneered.' Furthermore, in *Our Mutual Friend* a particularly odious and superficial couple are called 'Mr and Mrs Veneering'! Reason enough to see that the image of veneer was on its downward path.

The truth of the matter is that veneer must always go down on to a firm and stable ground. Today, chipboard and laminate boards are regarded as almost a cheap substitute for solid wood – the truth being that chipboard and laminates, manmade as they are, will stand up to modern heating and conditions in a way that solid wood cannot. They are in the 1980s the ideal materials for ground work, but they are far from cheap! For modern veneering I would select them every time. It's worth remembering that if veneer had not been developed we would not have laminate boards; try to imagine a world without plywood!

Toothing is a vital technique for the preparation of veneer. In the 1793 *Cabinet-makers London Book of Prices* veneering is charged for its preparation and laying; sawing is not mentioned. The masters supplied the veneer sawn, the journeymen prepared and laid it, and this preparation was known as toothing. It was a quick and simple way to remove the marks of sawing, and is why the evidence of sawing from the early days is so hard to find. The illustrations of this toothing show the point. The evidence of sawing (both freehand and with a guided saw) being such a rare thing to see, it is worth illustrating (photo 7–9). Because of this preparation veneers from these early days are never regular in their thickness, yet the accuracy of the mid-nineteenth-century veneers is striking and this can usually be seen.

Toothing was carried out with a plane that has a serrated cutting blade (diagram 11), the pressure required for its use being minimal when compared to that of a normal plane edge (photo 10–11). Vital for work on a delicate veneer, this toothing is often described as 'scoring' to create a good glueing surface. I do not believe that this was its purpose at all; more likely it was a fast and easy way to flatten the ground and remove the sawing kerfs from the veneer.

Today many exotic woods native to the Far East are rare, but in the 1500s, when the merchant venturers began to arrive in the East Indies, the first source of them, they would have been confronted with almost untouched growth. The major problems and cost would have been shipping the timber back to Europe fast enough. These woods were greatly prized; ebony was taxed and even marked or stamped to guarantee it as true ebony and not African blackwood or ebonised fruitwood (the practice of dyeing and black-varnishing). This practice might imply that ebony was rare, but this is unlikely to be the case,

photo 7

photo 8

photo 9

diagram 11

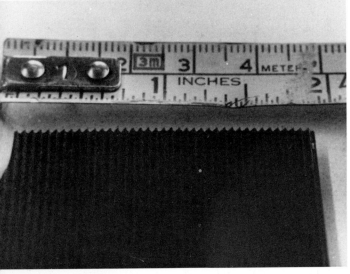

photo 10

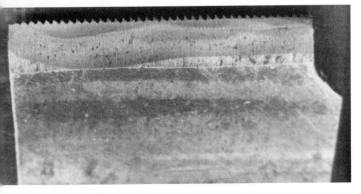

photo 11

mainly because of the huge quantity of ebony cabinets that have survived which must surely be a fraction of the total quantity produced. Indeed, if one wanted to reproduce cabinets or even a cabinet in these styles, it would be doubtful if a sufficiency of true ebony could be found – and the cost does not bear thinking about. But then in the sixteenth century, man had gone nothing like so far towards depleting Earth's natural resources.

The economy of modern veneering is extraordinary. Modern methods of cutting leave minimal wastage, and the surface of a veneer is so good that cleaning for finishing is hardly necessary.

We know that all veneers were sawn until the introduction of knife cutting around 1870. Even then, however, sawing did not die out; the finer and more exotic woods are still sawn and their cost is proportionately larger; in some cases ten times that of knife-work. My own stocks are mostly sawn, and they are almost without exception exotic.

Apart from the difficulty, sawing also produces sawdust. To create a veneer about 4mm ($\frac{3}{16}$ in) in thickness, it would be a fair assumption to say that at least 2mm–3mm of the wood must finish up on the floor as sawdust. A good craftsman in the eighteenth century was expected to saw eight veneers from one inch of wood! I am grateful to live in the twentieth century, as I could not perform such a prodigious feat, and considering that a veneer of 500mm (20 in) in width was not uncommon in the latter half of the eighteenth century, the feat of sawing eight veneers from a one-inch plank becomes even more astonishing, and without machinery almost impossible.

Sawing was time-consuming, and by modern standards wasteful of material, but it was the only way. Ebony – our first true veneer – with its hardness and peculiar properties, would have made the sawing even more difficult. It is of interest that on p. 230 of the *Cabinet-makers London Book of Prices*, we read that cabinet-makers charged more for working the hard, exotic woods. Again the book states on p. 9 that 'moulds and cauls [are] to be provided for the workman, or paid for according to time'. These items were vital for the laying of veneer.

Broadwood's Book of Square Piano Making includes

an engraving of a veneering shop from the late eighteenth century. A sturdy bench has resting on it the top board from a square piano which is to be veneered. On the left side of the workshop is a large hearth with a fire, and in front of this is the caul or board to be laid on the work. We can assume the work to be six feet long and two feet wide. The size and weight involved can be judged by the fact that the caul is attached by two chains from the roof beams! On the right the veneer is being glued by two boys, and the ground board by two more. The veneer is then placed on the ground, the glue allowed to cool, and the massive (and obviously very hot) caul is swung up and lowered down on to the veneer and ground. Bearers go across, struts from the roof beams are wedged on them, and the heat from the caul re-heats the glue, which is then squeezed out. Seven men and four boys were needed to veneer the top of a square piano. The hot iron and veneering hammer of today would have been useless for this sort of veneer.

What was the underlying reason for the development and use of veneer? The answer is again a simple one; veneer became a part of timber technology because it was the only way the new, exciting and exotic hardwoods like ebony could be successfully used. The properties of ebony make it difficult to work with: it is impossible to obtain a large piece of it, it is brittle and unstable and can crack at the slightest provocation; problems which in part also apply to the other hardwoods named as exotics. The only way to use the small logs of the exotic woods was as veneers.

Sawyers had been cutting their small fillets for inlays, and their techniques were now applied to ebony. For the first time a piece of furniture that was fully covered or veneered with a different wood made an appearance. The early methods for making small veneers are still there for us to see. The surface designs of the ebony cabinets of the seventeenth century are set up so that a large area of veneer is not necessary. They used the carver for decorative plaques and shaping capitals for columns, enjoying a material that responded to their skills in an almost magical way. The sheer density of the wood allowed a new

freedom to the woodworker; ebony workers developed new skills and became known as the 'Ebenistes'. From them the trade of cabinet-making originated.

The development of veneer was a huge step forward, yet realization of its full potential was slow. Almost one hundred years were to pass before natural decorative veneer was commonly employed. Veneer allowed the use of the diseased growth of trees, producing the extraordinary 'burr' or 'burl' surface. The crotch where branch meets trunk gave us the flame or curl veneer, root structures could be used, and trees pollarded for their saplings. All these parts of timber were previously discarded because of their frailty and instability in solid use, but could now come into their rightful place. With the development of the early mechanical frame and guided saws, larger and larger veneers appeared. When glued on to a firm and stable ground which held them together, these gave us the wonderful decorative surfaces of nature, and veneer an assured place in the history of furniture and the decorated surface. But the successful introduction of veneered ebony cabinets (photo 12) with their often superb carving and ripple of wave moulding – even at this time all cut by machine scrapers (photo 13), not just straight runs but compound shapes as well – still did not satisfy the demand for ornamentation, and the engraved ebony veneer was introduced.

Engraving is one of the oldest decorative techniques, from the earliest scratchings to the V cutting of wood, metal and stone, but the technique of the ebony cabinet is often quite different! Usually engraving is V cutting; sometimes the V is gilded or coloured to enhance it, with light surfaces often rubbed over with a mixture made from colouring, beeswax and rosin, filling it with black, red or other colours to show the pattern.

The ebony cabinet in the illustration was in my workshop for restoration. It is now in the Hamilton Palace room at the Boston Museum of Art, Massachusetts. In some areas during restoration re-engraving was necessary, and it was a surprise to find that this engraving was not V cut (diagram 12). It had been engraved with one vertical cut and another cut at 45° (diagram 13). The results

photo 12

photo 13

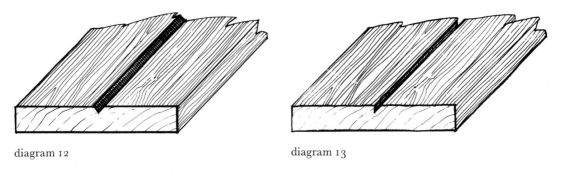

diagram 12   diagram 13

photo 14

20

photo 15

were astonishing. When I first saw this piece lit, it appeared as if it was inlaid with silver; photo 14 illustrates this effect. V engraving is as old as time and yet our ebony workers changed the rules and cut it as in diagram 13. To have engraved with a V tool would have been so much easier than the method chosen; it must follow that it was used purposely to obtain this dramatic effect.

Photo 15 shows a fine early portable backgammon box. All the techniques are here in a minute form, and it must be remembered that the smaller the piece, the more difficult the technique. The box when open is 350 × 640mm (14 × 26 in); the outside frame is of boxwood with light relief carving, painted and dyed to animate all the games and sports depicted. The dotting punch creates the 'C' scrollings, a predominant feature that will appear time and time again. The mitres show that the frame was carved and finished before being fitted around the box.

The backgammon board itself was in the beginning white and red; the red has now faded to brown. We can deduce this, since the dot punchings have been filled with red and black. The two panels of intarsia were laid first into the baseboard of limewood, and the knife marks can be seen at the tops of the triangles above and below the pictures where intarsia has been used. The overcutting of two woods for the pictures can be clearly seen. Heat or scorching (called sand shading) has been used for animation, and the inside frame has been cut from the inevitable ebony.

All that is needed for the next stage, marquetry, is represented in this charming gaming board. Veneer is treated in this case as a familiar technique, the tiny size of the box demonstrating the development of the saw. Designers and architects were becoming more and more adventurous and demanding, but the tradesmen, under their masters in the workshops, were equal to these demands. The development of their skills and ingenuity was rapid.

2

Marquetry

There is an enigma about this word as marquetry seems to be used to cover a variety of procedures. The dictionary states: 'Inlay, to set pieces of wood, metal etc. into a surface so that they are flush with it and form a design.' And for marquetry the definition reads; 'inlaid work in wood, ivory etc.'! Aesthetically there is no difference between inlay and marquetry, but technically there is. With marquetry the ground used is veneer instead of solid wood; this makes it possible to create the whole decoration and prepare it for laying as if it were a veneer, with all the advantages that this will bring. Marquetry can easily be made to cover shaped surfaces, creating intricate patterns; and since the basic tool is the saw, the process can be likened to drawing pictures with a saw.

If we refer back to the different types of sawing wood mentioned in the previous chapter, the basic principle of marquetry is the 'sandwich' method. As an example, the ebony cabinet when opened revealed a centre cupboard of which the whole surface is a veneer, not inlaid into the solid wood (photo 16).

Behind this arch is a relevant example (photo 17), the drawer faces having been cut just as the bog oak and holly were. The difference is that these drawer faces are veneered. The positive and negative effect can be clearly seen, and the production of two surfaces through one process of sawing has been achieved.

The design of the saw that cut this work had been improved vastly over the preceeding 25 years. This example dates from c. 1650. I have never seen a saw blade from this period and would be delighted if I could; but one thing is certain, seventeenth-century craftsmen could make use of a very thin type of saw – and a guess can be made at the depth, since this governs the tightness of curve and scroll in a design. Similarly, depth of blade will govern whether the saw can be turned to come back out of a cut – something which in early work it rarely seems to do. All these factors will affect the intricacy of a design.

Saw blades were hand-made and when a modern fretsaw blade is examined it is difficult to imagine how a comparable blade could be made by hand. It should be remembered that the capability existed to hammer or blanish metal to this degree of delicacy; clock springs from the time carry the ideal thickness and when examined will show the draw filing used to finish them. This would be an ideal material, and once a saw vise to hold such a fine blade was produced, the cutting of the teeth would be a simple matter. Many fine saws have been made in my own workshop, the sharpening carried out by filing straight across the blade. On the first cut alternate teeth are filed: on reversing the blade in the vise the teeth between are cut (diagram 14). Filing straight across will usually put the necessary set for clearance on the cutting edge. In practice files do not have the sharp edges shown in the diagram; the apex of the files leave a round impression. Hardening and tempering – being understood from the earliest times – would present no problems, if indeed this was necessary at all in making wood-saws.

The fineness of these saws would present prob-

photo 16

lems if it was necessary to cut one by hand today – and the cost would be unacceptable. In the late eighteenth century, clock and watchmakers made chains so fine that an eyeglass is needed to see that they are in fact chains at all, and that every link has been riveted – yet the job was carried out by children! Young apprentices would have first learned tool-maintenance in the marquetry shops – simpler jobs such as these were too mundane to assign to the craftsmen. Nevertheless, many marquetry saws break before becoming dull.

The saw can only be used when a design has been made for cutting. It is often said that the very nature of marquetry work destroys the design, and so it must; but it is vital that copies of the design can be made, as they will be needed later for reference. Often a way of repeating the master

pattern was required to run off copies! To reduce the expense of this, the answer was age-old and simple: needle pricking. Today there are other alternatives: photography, photocopying, and printing, yet this early method is still widely used.

The drawing (photo 18) is of a tulip to be made of two contrasting veneers. The drawn lines have been needle-pricked on to a paper beneath, and the result is a permanent perforated copy of the design (photo 19). The finest linen paper was used. This perforated pattern could be employed to create copies, allowing the master to be kept.

Copies were made by the use of a pounce – made up as a felt roll, or teased cotton or wool covered with fine linen and filled with asphaltum, bitumen or fine carbon dust (diagram 15 shows the latter), and a simple awl for pricking. This,

photo 17

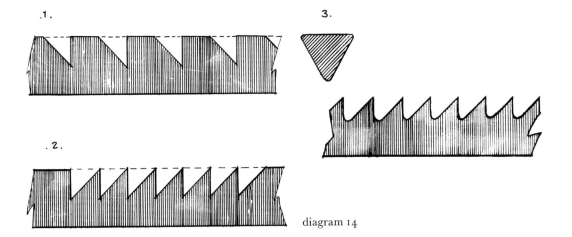

.1.

.2.

3.

diagram 14

photo 18

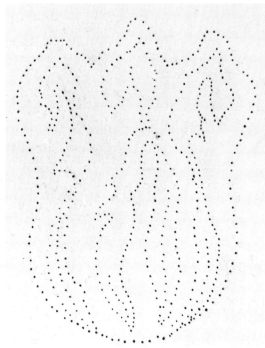

photo 19

when pounced or gently pounded over the perforated pattern on to a paper beneath, would leave a precise pattern, which, with heat, could be fixed and an accurate copy produced. As many copies as needed could be taken – perhaps the derivation of the carbon papers of today! (photo 20). So important was this function that hand-operated pricking machines were in common use in the marquetry workshops (diagram 16). The needle is still favoured (see *Fine Woodworking*, April 1981 p. 47), as it is a sure and easy method when power cuts, breakdowns or lack of copying papers cause modern technology to fail. Using this method and keeping the original designs is how repetition was made possible through the years.

We now have a pattern and a saw blade, but a means of holding the blade is still needed. Photos 21 and 22 show a modern coping and piercing saw, the solution for probably the past four hundred years. With practice they will follow all the shapes asked of them. The same is true of the small and familiar treadle fretsaw (diagram 17). Both the fretsaw and piercing saw are designed to

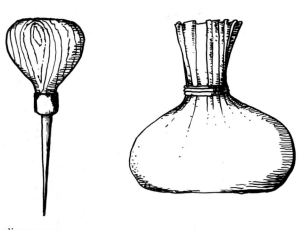

diagram 15

cut vertically, and it has always surprised me to see illustrations of eighteenth-century cutters using the saw horizontally. They chose a difficult way to execute their work (photo 23).

This traditional method of sawing has always intrigued me. In the beginning it would have made the work difficult and tiring, but, as with all

25

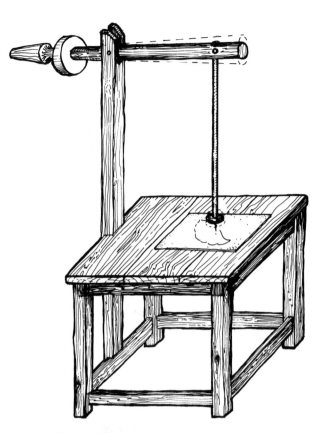

diagram 16

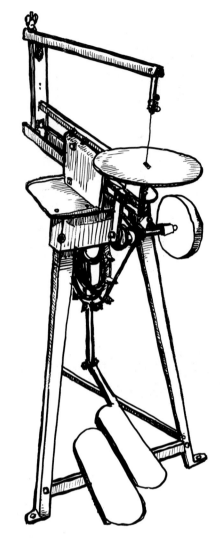

diagram 17

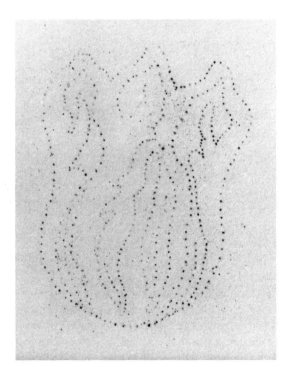

photo 20

things, this would have become an accepted part of the trade. The illustration of the man at his machine, called the 'donkey' or 'cutter's vise', does not show the fineness of the saw blade being used; however the similarity of the frame of his saw to a coping saw is amazing, and this saw is used horizontally.

How did the vise come to evolve in this way? In the illustration showing the donkey, the presence of the vise may raise queries. This was very much the traditional vise of the wood-carver, and the coping saw (invented about 1575) was often used with the work held vertically. Put these consider-

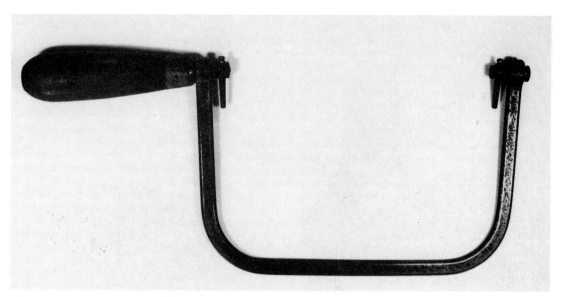

photo 21

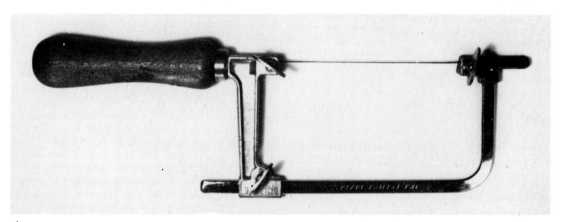

photo 22

ations together, and the reason for the donkey becomes clear. A further reason is that this method allows the maximum amount of daylight to be utilized (photo 24). This was a major reason for the further development of the donkey: with the easy light-availability that we have today it is difficult to accept the huge problems there must have been three hundred and fifty years ago.

The modern steel-framed fretsaw is compressed and the saw then clamped into position; the pressure on the frame is then released. Tension on the blade is automatic. The size of work is governed by the depth of the gooseneck or throat of the saw, and the size of work that can be comfortably held must be considered; this was without doubt a factor governing the size of the saw frame. The early frames, and indeed all donkey-frames, are made of wood, the spring of the frame created by laying long-grain wood across the short grain at the neck end of the frame. The saw blades were held in place as they are today; it is astounding how many things do not change.

The illustration of the cutter at his donkey shows he is using the saw freehand; the weakness of this method can be seen in the two drawers of

photo 23

photo 24

the ebony cabinet. The fit from one to the other is not very good. The secret of good marquetry is the ability to saw at exactly 90° to the work or veneers (diagram 18 illustrates the point); allow the cut to wander from exactly 90° and you will either have a loose fit, or no fit at all. Over and over again examples of marquetry demonstrate this problem. The answer was not long in coming; the donkey was developed and the saw frame put into guides that ensure cutting at 90° – or very near – to the work (diagram 19). The date of this development is hard to fix; I would place it in the second half of the eighteenth century.

Diagram 19 shows a modern cutter's donkey. The saw guides guarantee a 90° cut through the work and the rockers allow a movement of the saw through almost 300°. This is most important, and helps to alleviate the continuous movement of the work by the operator's left hand. The bar below the frame is adjustable for different sizes of saw

frame and also reversible for the convenience of left-handed operators!

The method of operation is simple. The veneers to be cut are joined together (the pattern fixed to the veneer facing the seat) and then the foot puts pressure on the jaws of the vise holding the veneers. The saw blade is threaded through the work if necessary, or otherwise starts from the outside. The cutting edge of the saw can point downward, left or right, and can now be moved back and forth in its guides; the foot pressure is eased so that the pattern can be positioned around the moving blade until all the pattern has been cut.

The sandwich of veneers (called a 'parcel') is the basic technique of sawn marquetry – the beauty of the idea being that even if the design was not followed exactly, a near perfect fit would result. The simplicity of the idea allows for outstanding work of such artistry that it can defy satisfactory description, as colour plates (i) and (ii) of a table-top from *c.* 1685 to 1690 will show.

Three veneers have been used for decoration. At this stage I have not written about the ground veneer (in this case ebony) and it is better to think of the decoration only. When the direction of grain is examined, it can be seen that in certain places the fits are not all that they should be; at least three different sawings have been used to achieve the effect. The complexity of this piece of floral marquetry is amazing, and I was privileged to be responsible for its restoration. Whoever cut it was a genius. However, at the top of colour plate (i) a narcissus surrounded with laurel buds can be seen, and a one-veneer tulip is laid in; it rests in solitary state, no stalk attaching it to the flora around it. A feature of design? I doubt it. It seems that even a genius can forget to add a stalk.

We have examined examples of the finest marquetry. There is no better way to show how this parcel cutting is done than to take some work apart and see the evidence of the saw and the craftsman's ability to control it.

Photo 25 shows a tulip from a large marquetry panel; it is two-veneer sawn and dates from *c.* 1688. The saw width can be judged by the obvious problems experienced turning corners; nowhere can the saw be seen to have been turned to come back out of the cut. Instead, this has been accomplished by moving back a little and then turning; the thickness at points marked with a cross show this turning-point, and the problems of sawing in a clean line can be clearly seen. The sawyer is given great licence in his accuracy through this method, and it is also possible to trace the set of the saw as it moved through the work.

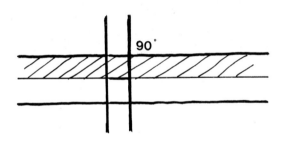

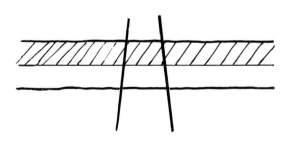

diagram 18

· a·treadle.
· b·seat.
· c·saw frame.
· d·rockers
· e·fixed jaw.
· f·moving jaw.
· g·saw blade

cutting donkey.

diagram 19

photo 25

photo 26

At this stage another point must be raised; the technique of marquetry can be 'read', and the inference does seem to be made that sometimes as many as eight veneers may have been cut at the one sawing. Herbert Cescinsky, who writes, in *The Gentle Art of Faking Furniture*, with authority and understanding, has nevertheless never tried to saw eight veneers of the same thickness as the work now being illustrated. Cescinsky claims that this fine marquetry saw was cutting a shape of 25mm (1 in) thickness. I feel this would have been impossible – as a rule – in marquetry from the seventeenth and eighteenth centuries; three veneers of such a thickness cut at the one time is the maximum. This can be illustrated with countless examples.

The veneer thickness in our example is 3mm ($\frac{1}{8}$ in) after being cleaned-up and finished (photo 26); its intitial thickness must have been considerably more. During the repair of this piece of marquetry it became necessary to saw and create our own veneer. To produce a veneer to finish as in photo 26, a full millimetre was needed for

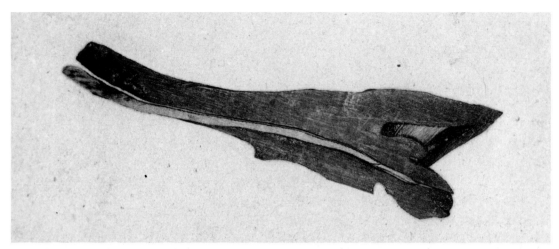

photo 27

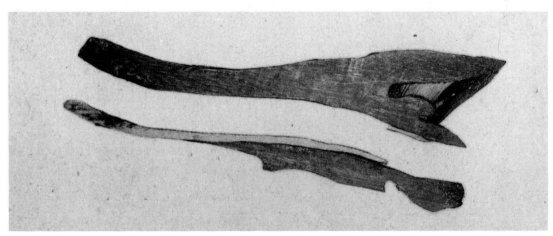

photo 28

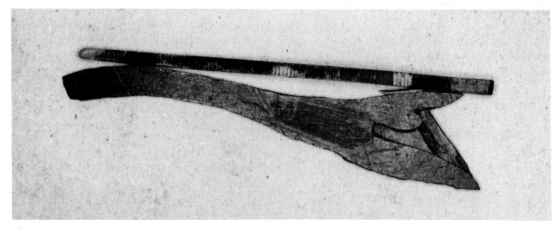

photo 29

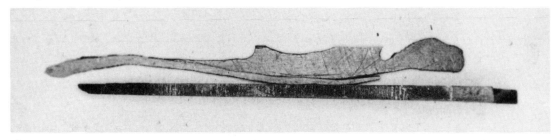

photo 30

photo 31

photo 32

preparation and cleaning up, and it can be safely assumed that the veneers in this sample would have been 4mm–5mm ($\frac{3}{16}$ in) when they left the saw in 1688.

The illustrations that follow showing the parcel-cutting of these heavy veneers are rare, even unique. The tulip was made from sabecu and boxwood, as is the small piece of work (photo 27) from the same panel, c. 1688. Its length is 75mm (3 in) long. The dark sabecu, the light boxwood, and the set of the saw can all be seen. With photo 28 the join is separated and in photo 29 the boxwood is turned on edge, where the sawing marks can be seen. (The dark areas, incidentally, are glue that has moved up the join when the surface was laid). Similarly, photo 30 shows the sabecu that has lain alongside, and the sawing

again can be seen. Photos 31 and 32 are of the box and sabecu enlarged, and give a clear indication that they were sawn together at the same time.

From the same source is photo 33. Again the set of the saw can be followed and this, when taken apart and compared, reveals the same technique. But with photo 34 the scale can be judged by the thumb and forefinger; we are looking at the vertical sawn line at the left of photo 33.

The technique, if used in this manner, can be tried by anybody; the pitfalls are few and any that do arise will almost certainly be the result of the veneers themselves not being suitable for the process. They must be dense and pliable – not of the rotary cut or peeled variety, but of the true knife-cut or sawn type and also as thick as it is possible to obtain.

A list of suitable woods is open to discussion, but might include box, holly, sycamore or maple, thuya, walnut, tulipwood, kingwood, some rosewoods, purpleheart, sabecu, satinwood, hawthorn, bog oak, and ebony. The holly and sycamore are most useful because of their ability to be stained to a multitude of colours. The golden rule is to ascertain that the wood is dense and not brittle; a good test is to see if when cut to a fine point across the grain, the point remains. It is unlikely that anyone reading this book will be using woods for the purposes of commercial marquetry, and the modern process will not be of use to those wishing to create a picture, or repair or restore existing work. However, the principle is basically the same; the difference is in the sawing. The commercial sawing has to be exact and is dependent on the skill of the sawyer, since the sandwich cut is not used.

In fact, true machinery is used, deep-throated powered jig-saws, or a large table saw, with the top of the saw ceiling-suspended so that the depth of throat is not a limitation. The saw blade is between 0.015 and 0.018 in thick and is hand-sharpened (again sharpened straight across, the

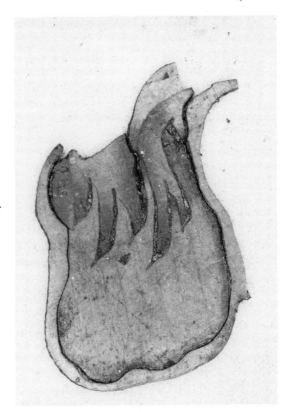

photo 33

photo 34

33

filing creating the 'set' or clearance on the saw.) This practice will also successfully set the teeth for very fine band-saws.

Sawing begins with a pattern, the various woods and colours of the pattern marked. Perhaps surprisingly, the pricked design method is still favoured (see *Fine Woodworking*, April 1981, p. 47). Should we decide to make the tulip (in photo 18) using this method the process is as follows: make up two separate parcels of veneer, (of say twenty), well within the scope of a modern machine. A bundle of twenty boxwood veneers is laid up; and a thin plywood is placed below the veneer and another on top to carry the pattern. The bundle is clenched together with panel pins. A similar bundle of purpleheart veneers is made up before sawing can commence. It remains for the sawyer's skill to split the lines of the marking with his blade – the ideal situation being when the line runs down the V of the saw set (diagram 20) – something which is obviously not always possible. When both have been sawn and the desired degree of accuracy achieved – and this accuracy must be within the thickness of the saw – the bundles are separated, animated and the pieces assembled one into the other. This method enables complicated pictures to be made up in surprising quantity (see *Fine Woodworking*, April 1981, p. 46). Such is commercial production, and the jig-saw with its large table and limitless throat enables large-scale marquetry to be undertaken.

Large areas of intarsia were not uncommon during the fifteenth, sixteenth and seventeenth centuries; whole rooms were decorated with the technique. Large areas of sawn marquetry would have presented a different problem, and yet they exist. *Christies International Review*, September/October 1984 featured a superb and rare example of a pair of wall panels, measuring 1.83 m (6 ft) by 1.15 m (3 ft 9 in); the birds are lifesize and the date is 1688. These were the source of the marquetry used to demonstrate parcel sawing.

All the work is sawn, and no evidence of inlay can be found. If the sawing of the marquetry followed the assumed method of horizontal cutting, some areas of work would have been so heavy that it would have been impossible to support them without assistance. It has been

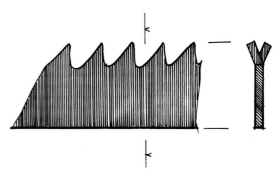

diagram 20

suggested that it was the task of the apprentice to support the work during cutting! The logical and simple method would have been to saw the work vertically, and during repair this was the method used. A simple way to create this very large scale of work would be to use the rear-pivoted frame-saw (diagram 21), a very early method of fret-cutting and the ancestor of the treadle-fret and jig-saw. Another likely answer would be the treadle-frame saw (diagram 22). These were in common use during the eighteenth century; not just small treadle versions such as this, but large frames with multiple saws, for use in mills in the commercial production of sawn timber. Leonardo da Vinci designed one, and a model is in the Museum of Science in Milan. Similarly, a mill with a multiple bank of saws still operates as a tourist attraction near Arnhem in the Netherlands, dated 1621.

We now come to *Animation*, the 'life and soul' of marquetry. 'Sand-burning', 'sand-scorching', 'sand-shading'; animation is called all of these, but can be likened quite simply to toasting. In the days of the fork you governed how your bread was toasted; modern electric toasters do this for themselves with different degrees of heat.

The material used for the process is vital. It must be silver sand of not-too-fine a consistency. A convenient container, or heavy iron plate, and a means of heating the container and sand are also necessary. Of all the processes of marquetry, animation is the only one that needs more than sheer skill. Artistry can make or break the whole process. The size of the pieces may be miniscule, yet each must be shaded to a greater or lesser degree. Another vital factor is the quality of the veneer itself; the denser the better. Box is a wonderful adapter, and sycamore and holly also. The rule is, the paler and denser the wood, the better will be the shading.

Times change very little; the only difference in photos 35 and 36 is that the heat source has changed from charcoal to electricity – and the style of clothing. The results on the boxwood piece held in pliers would be the same; the shading when removed from the heat of the sand can be seen. Over zealous use of heat shows in photo 37; it should be gradual: too much heat and charring can happen very quickly. One useful alternative is to use the heat for a complete colour change. Photo 38 is a sand tray, and in photo 39 a piece of East Indian satinwood has been laid upon it. This veneer is $1\frac{1}{2}$mm thick and has been 'toasted' for two minutes; it has turned a permanent rich golden-brown tone from its original butter colour (photo 40). This technique can be used to bring certain veneers to near blackness in colour; in photo 43 the leaves are made from pearwood. Sometimes diseased wood is used, but not in this instance – no evidence of disease could be found, and the texture of the veneer was consistent with the hardest charcoal.

Strange as it may seem, animation work was always achieved with saw-and-sand shading until about 1760, when engraving of work began. Photo 42 shows the left-hand panel of a table by Thomas Chippendale from about 1770, which has been engraved using the knife. (Photo 106 shows the centre panel). The tiny harebells in the ovals are three individual pieces of wood, each shaded and engraved; the engraving on the acanthus is almost hesitant and weak. This is a very important surface since the engraving, apart from the restored areas, is a rare original. Compare this with the boldness of photo 41, a work completed twelve years later. The engraving here is everything, and no shading is used. The reasons given for this change have been many; but in my opinion there is only one: speed. In fact, the next stage, penwork, was not long in arriving. Black ink and a fine lining pen, used after the first coat of varnish, became the accepted practice; this al-

diagram 21

diagram 22

lowed such fine detail that in a short time the basic simplicity of marquetry was lost. I believe it was this, and not simply a change in fashion, that brought about the decline of the art.

How to engrave marquetry is up to the individual. My own favourite method is to mark the work with a pencil and then cut it with a knife. The use of woodcut engraving tools is difficult because of the size of work. Use a knife, or whatever is comfortable. A centre cut, with a cut above 10° to either side will, after practice, produce the desired effect; this can be enhanced with fillers, as in photo 41. But I have found fillers are not necessary in most cases, and prefer the engravings to be filled during the process of polishing, unless of course coloured fillers are desired – and are used as part of the design.

These are the basic principles of marquetry. The saw, being paramount in development, never seemed to decline in use on the Continent. The illustrations need no further words from me, except to say today one never sees these articles in their full and intended colour; age dulls the surface and they fade to a uniform gold. When you see a floral panel which has not been touched since it was made, it can be hard to believe that when new the panel was as colourful as nature. In my work of repair and restoration, complete

photo 35

photo 36

photo 37

photo 38

photo 39

photo 40

photo 41

photo 42

panels of marquetry sometimes have to be removed. The reasons are many; worm, rot, or severe warping have often necessitated such a radical step. These old surfaces carry a useful secret in the glue line. Where the veneer joins the ground, the original colour can always be found. These colours were often the colours of nature; it is perhaps sad that photographic records are not always kept.

The colouring of woods was not an early practice; leaves were usually cut from bone or ivory in the beginning, then dyed green. The tendency to use colour was nevertheless present from the outset and gradually the dyeing of the veneer itself began. I have heard it suggested that dyeing usually began after the shape was cut, but I do not agree with this. As today, a whole piece of veneer would more probably have been coloured before cutting began. Incidentally, the colour is often retained around the sawcut of a flower. This is not deliberate, but shows where the glue in the sawcut has (as with the glue line) retained the colour of the dye.

I know little about the dyeing methods used on seventeenth- and eighteenth-century woods. There is, however, one interesting point; the

woods dyed are without exception of whitish variety and reasonably fast-growing; sycamore, poplar, plane and holly being favourites. Considering the thickness of the veneers in those days, dyeing of them would have created many problems. The obvious solution was to change the colour of the tree. It was this practice which created harewood: the sycamore was injected with ferrous oxide in the root structures, one to two years before felling, which changed the colour to a silvery grey. In the same way, the hydrangea flower is naturally pink until some iron is put amongst the roots, when the flowers will become a silvery blue.

This subject was discussed during a lecture in America. Three weeks later the following was sent to me:

Colouring Wood
French cabinet makers can now make wood of any colour they please, by letting the roots of the trees absorb the coloured fluids the year before it is cut down. A solution of iron passed up one root, and of prussiate of potash up the other, will give the wood a permanent blue colour.*

As I have said this was an obvious solution before the advent of the fast and permanent colourings such as aniline during the last half of the nineteenth century. I am grateful to Mrs Laurent J. Torno Jnr. of St Louis for her interest.

The colours when new of these seventeenth- and eighteenth-century surfaces can only now be imagined. The skills attained by the marqueteurs were remarkable. Their basic techniques were simple, but the results often amazing. Yet having reached such a point in skill the life of marquetry was to be short lived; we shall now see how rapid was the advance of machinery and mass production.

* *Scientific American*, New York, vol. 3, no. 37, 3 June 1848, p. 296.

photo 43

−3

Parquetry, oyster work, bandings and Tunbridgeware

Unlike marquetry, the origins of parquetry can be traced. It seems to originate from the word *parque*, to make an enclosure of land; the formal and regular pattern of gardens within these enclosures existed before the familiar parquet floor. A *parqueteur* is a floor-layer and parquetry can be easily explained as an inlaid or veneered surface which depends upon geometric shapes.

Parquetry relies almost entirely on the straight line. In furniture, perhaps the simplest form is the quartered top and herring-bone inlay, in walnut-veneered furniture of the early eighteenth century. In the beginning it was common practice to lay the main veneer and then each veneer of different grain-direction was laid up to it. In photo 44, which is a walnut drawer-front from *c*.1720, this can be seen. After the walnut veneer is removed the surface toothing is very evident. The line of the cutting gauge is still distinct, and even the scraping-off of the toothing during the waste veneer removal (before the first feather of walnut was laid in place). It is possible not only to see the cutting-back of the first feather, but also the second and even the cut to receive the cross-bands; as in photo 45, where the corner has been turned at the end of the drawer.

Feathering has been used to a great degree almost since veneering began. The method is to cut the veneer at an angle of 45° to the grain direction. Feathering reached a decorative peak during the eighteenth century, as the German commode in photo 46 shows. However, the heaviness of the feathering shown here is the exception rather than the rule.

Feathering led to a fortunate discovery: to lay a quartered top of four matching veneers, four consecutive veneers from the same log can be used. The object of the exercise is to make the pattern symetrical, especially if one corner of each veneer is decorative, as in diagram 23; the bottom right corner being in this the decorative one. This type of pattern can only work if leaf A is laid first, then leaf B must be turned over before it can be laid; C is laid the same way as A, D must be turned over as was leaf B (diagram 24). This simple technique is used for quartering in all its applications. When applied to feathering patterns it allows for the variegations of colour that can so often be seen, and which show up quite dramatically with the German commode.

Photo 47 shows a drawer of French manufacture, 1710–1720, and again shows this variegation perfectly. The drawer is veneered with East Indian rosewood which, when new, is almost black. The photograph shows the handles removed, and very little variegation is visible. In fact, the difference in colour does not fully show until the veneers have faded, which raises an interesting point. Did early cabinet-makers and veneerers know this was going to happen? Most of the early veneers were very dark indeed. They also fade very quickly, the darkness of the wood being a natural foil for the gilded mounts that much of this furniture carried. Scraping to bring back the colour was the order of the day, and this is presumably the reason why so many articles that have survived have paper-thin but original veneers remaining.

photo 44

photo 45

photo 46

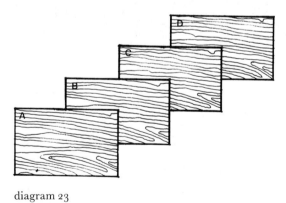

diagram 23

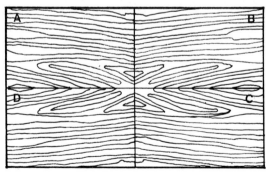

diagram 24

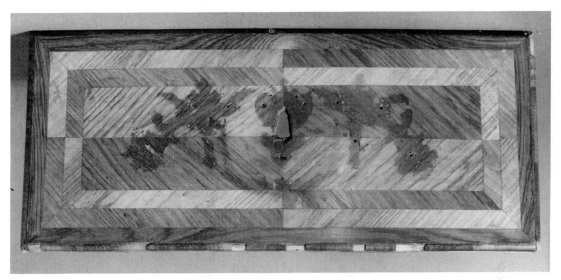

photo 47

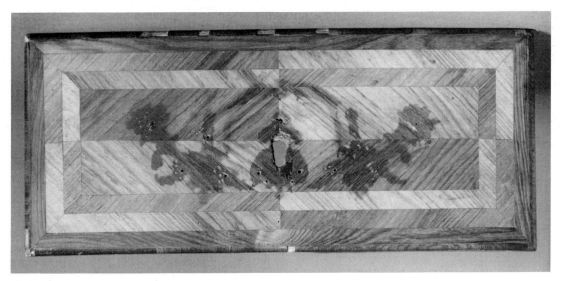

photo 48

This question of veneer reversal can be illustrated by the drawer from photo 47. All that has happened in photo 48 is that the drawer has been turned over: the change of colour can be seen perfectly.

There is a table made by Thomas Chippendale in 1772 at Nostel Priory in Yorkshire which illustrates this point perfectly. It is a gaming table, and its drawer has spent many years of its life half open. Light and atmosphere have bleached out the colour, making a dramatic contrast with the original colour in the back half of the backgammon board. Similarly, when looking at the faded half, one quarter stands out as much darker than the other three. Without doubt it has been reversed, while its opposite leaf has not. If variegation is not required, then any form of quartering should be excluded from the design, since the alteration of grain direction or its reversal are the basis of almost all forms of parquetry.

45

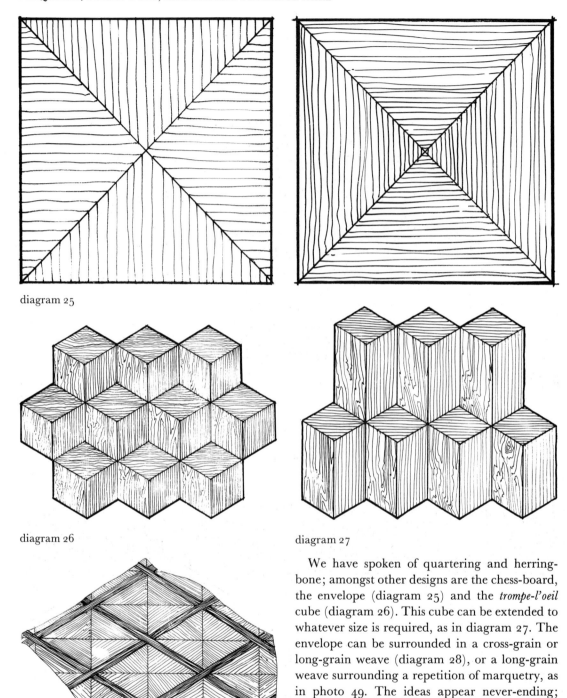

diagram 25

diagram 26

diagram 27

diagram 28

We have spoken of quartering and herring-bone; amongst other designs are the chess-board, the envelope (diagram 25) and the *trompe-l'oeil* cube (diagram 26). This cube can be extended to whatever size is required, as in diagram 27. The envelope can be surrounded in a cross-grain or long-grain weave (diagram 28), or a long-grain weave surrounding a repetition of marquetry, as in photo 49. The ideas appear never-ending; photos 50, 51, 52, and 53 show this simple principle of using angles of grain direction against each other. The reversal of veneer can create surfaces that appear to have many different species of timber selected for effect, but this is not

photo 49

photo 50

photo 51

photo 52

the case with photos 50 and 51. Here, one species of timber has been used for the surface; in photos 52 and 53 the number is only three. However, the important thing is accuracy – no matter how simple the idea or drawing – otherwise the end result does not work. Methods also need to be found for accurate reproduction of the pieces.

For this job knives are not recommended; and saw combined with jig is without doubt the best technique. A very fine dovetail-saw or a gentleman's pad-saw is ideal for this work, and the ability to sharpen and set it correctly is vital. Time spent on achieving this is still worth every second. Parquetry is geometrical, so jigs that will automatically create angles are the answer to almost all of its problems.

Diagrams 26 and 27 of *trompe l'oeil* are probably the most well-know form of the technique. All the pieces are diamonds or parallelograms, with their largest angle 120°. A simple mitre box to cut this

angle is made up (photo 54); and a gate to govern the size of pieces (photos 55 and 56). This is a jig that can be adapted to cut the necessary pieces for all straight-line geometric parquetry.

Three veneers are necessary and these are prepared to the correct width for the pattern. This width is set in the jig shown in photo 54, the necessary number of pieces are sawn (photo 57), and then assembled (photo 58). This assembly can take many forms: the simplest is to glue the patterns on to paper, as shown here, and then lay them in a single operation. The two assembled sheets (photos 59 and 60) can be prepared and laid. It is worth drawing attention to the way in which the grain direction of two pieces has been altered. This point must be watched; the difference in colour can be noticed even at this stage.

This method of making and using jigs has not changed over the generations. Photo 61 is from *c*.1770; the shooting board being used to plane the

49

photo 53

photo 54

photo 55

photo 56

photo 57

photo 58

photo 59

photo 60

veneer edge and the cutting gauge to make the veneer strips (photo 62). In illustration 61 there is one piece of equipment hardly seen today; the stripping-plane at the top right-hand corner. Today, fillets of box, ebony, rosewood and sycamore, amongst others, are sawn to a remarkable accuracy, 1mm ($\frac{1}{26}$ in) square being the smallest. This accuracy shows immediately when compared with the hand pulled fillets from an earlier era. The fineness achieved is quite remarkable, as photo 63 shows. The total accuracy of the machine can always be favourably compared with the human hand, a fact not always understood when the appraisal of articles is considered. Compare photo 63 with photo 64, which dates from 1850.

The cutting gauge is a useful form of knife not only for its ease of use, but also for its safety! Illustrations showing modern trimming-knives and steel straight-edges for cutting veneer should be discounted (diagram 29). The smallest burr on a steel edge can cause the knife to run off, and the accidents can be nasty. If a straight edge is the only way, use one of hardwood, 4mm ($\frac{3}{16}$ in) thick, and always, if possible, clamp it in place and keep the free hand *behind* the cutting edge.

All parquetry depends very much on wood colour and contrast (colour plate (iv)), so with the huge selection of veneers available today some wonderful effects can be created. Parquetry will combine with marquetry in many ways; the use of french curves combined with a two-wood envelope produced the surfaces of the small night table in photo 65. Always remember the consequences of veneer reversal. It is workshop practice to mark the face of veneers with chalk so that veneer reversal is always on purpose, not accidental. There is nothing worse than creating a pattern which when finished and polished, turns out to have one piece in a totally different colour!

54

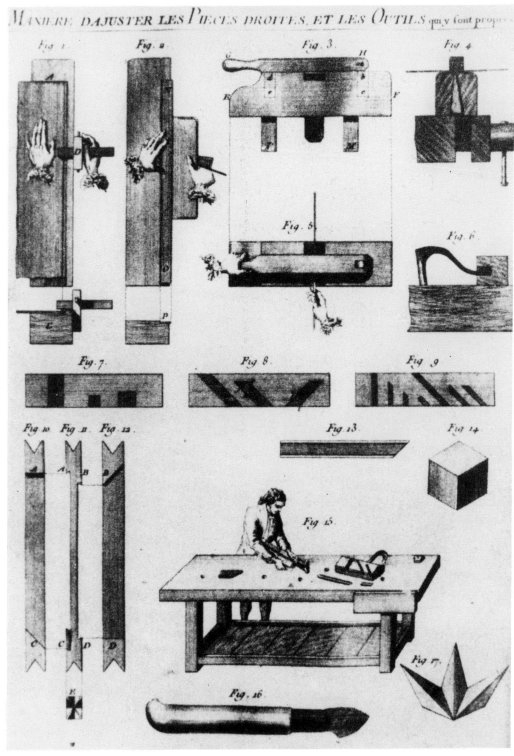

photo 61

photo 62

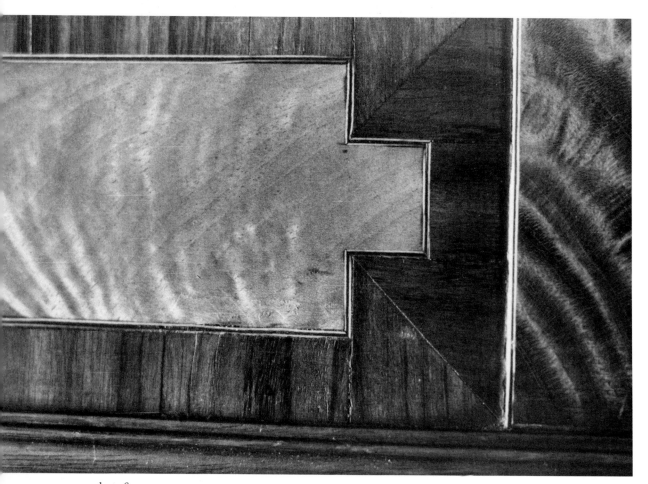

photo 63

photo 64   photo 65

diagram 29

Oyster work

Oyster work or oyster pieces can cause problems.
The oyster – a veneer sawn across the grain – is cut
traditionally from walnut, olive, laburnum, kingwood, tulipwood, *lignum vitae* or yew. The reason
for its use is difficult to understand until the size of
a normal oyster is taken into consideration. They
are cut from wood too small for normal veneer
sawing. Photo 66 shows an oyster from a tamarisk
root which is almost a briar, and very decorative

photo 66

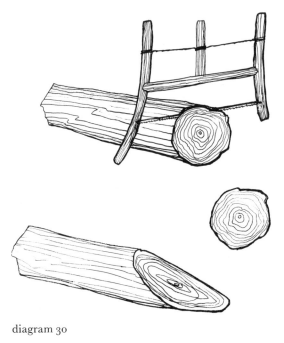

diagram 30

and dense in its cross-grain structure. It is also very adaptable for replacement work.

Another variation is the butterfly cut; sawing at 45° to the grain (diagram 30). But oyster and butterfly cuts can produce problems; the natural fragility of wood when it is of such short grain should need no explanation. This obviously cuts down the selection of woods which can be used, and the demand for them today is minimal; most people who want to carry out this technique will probably find it advantageous to saw their own.

Timber selection for the oyster or butterfly cut is vital. I have said that almost any timber can be used, and so it can, but it must be stable, seasoned, and carry minimal starring in the centre of the end grain. These qualities are in themselves hard to find, but the veneer will also have to be much thicker than normal.

Once the material is available, the method of sawing the veneer must be chosen. Hand-sawing is probably the best, a bandsaw next choice, and I would put the circular saw last. After each saw-

photo 67

cut, prepare the sawn surface for laying as a veneer. This will be more difficult to do when it is complete. The same rules apply for cutting a butterfly; these, incidentally, are rather more difficult than oysters.

My own method for cutting oysters, mainly to produce them quickly and with accuracy, is to make up the jig shown in photo 67. All that has been done is to take the principle of the frame-saw and add handles to it, and then turn the cutting edge to the horizontal. It makes a fast and very accurate guided saw. Similarly, a large picture-frame mitre-saw can be adapted for the purpose.

Having obtained a supply of oyster and butterfly pieces, parquetry can commence. The easiest way is to lay in squares (diagram 31), or brickwall them (diagram 32). The best way is to lay them as hexagons, from which the honeycomb pattern results (diagram 33). The octagon is another approach, making a square infill of a contrasting wood (diagram 34). Thought can be given here to producing accurately a long-grain

diagram 31

diagram 32

diagram 33

this can be seen on furniture from the late seventeenth century, as at Ham House.

It is interesting that the oyster-work from the seventeenth century became the parquetry work of the eighteenth century – the designs in so many instances being similar, if not identical. The use of oysters ran its course, fashion and designs changed, end-grain veneers being used to a lesser and lesser degree. They did appear again during the eighteenth century on some of the finest work, the ebeniste Bernhard van Reisenburg (BVRB) being probably the finest exponent of it. They appear in marquetry known as *Bois d'bout*, and the floral work of end-cut kingwood set into a ground of satinee, producing a beautiful effect (photo 68). This piece carries the mark of the master BVRB *c.* 1750.

Parquetry, as with so many designs and styles, ran its course of popularity. It also created along the way decorative banding; that is to say, the cross-band laid into a single string-line of ivory, ebony, box and herringbone. The herringbone of photo 44 shows how the bandings were built up on the work, a slow and tedious method. Photo 61,

diagram 34

billet with a square, hexagon, or octagon shape, before sawing across the grain begins. This will help greatly in the accurate sawing of veneers and become a huge advantage when the laying of the surface begins.

The butterfly veneer can be used by alternating the grain direction of one piece against another. This produces a watered-silk appearance and can be used to good effect as a cross banding for an oyster-veneered surface (diagram 35). The most startling of all is the full butterfly pattern. Twelve leaves make the centre circle, a silk effect cross-band is sawn into this – surrounded by a simple square oyster – shaped into the corner quadrants and also cross-banded (diagram 36). Examples of

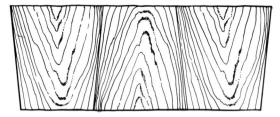

diagram 35

diagram 36

from 1770, shows the next stage in making up single lengths of banding for decoration. The answer was not long in arriving and depended very much on machines and the ability to produce blocks of different woods glued together, usually with a veneer on either side from which a series of finished bands could be sawn; almost like ply-woods with decorative cores.

If we take a piece of ebony 150mm (6 in) wide, 600mm (24 in) long, and 3mm ($\frac{1}{8}$ in) thick, and glue on either side of it a piece of boxwood having the same dimensions, when dry we have a ply-

photo 68

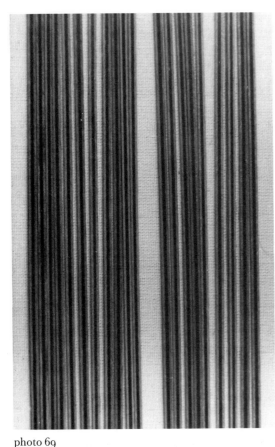

photo 69

wood of white-black-white, with the grains running in the same direction. This can now be sawn into white-black-white strips – although on a much finer scale. Photo 69 shows the result.

Similarly, photo 70 is of a feather banding 20mm ($\frac{3}{4}$ in) wide. It is the top of a block when sawn through and through and the result is photo 71. The veneer top and bottom is a guard strip and is usually removed before laying: beware the 'antique' with this still in place! Similarly, photo 72 shows the effect with a check-banding block when sawn through and through.

The making of blocks can be complicated, with many glueings and sawings needed to complete our 'plywood' for the bandings. Diagram 37 shows the initial sawing for the production of a feather band. Similarly, with diagram 38, the creation of a two-colour feather begins with this initial glueing, before sawing and assembly into a band can begin.

The diversity and complexity of some bandings is extraordinary, and sometimes the results unfortunate, as the writing-box from 1870 in photo 72a shows. Band-making progressed and the idea was extended and re-appears in another technique, which makes the original pale into insignificance.

photo 70

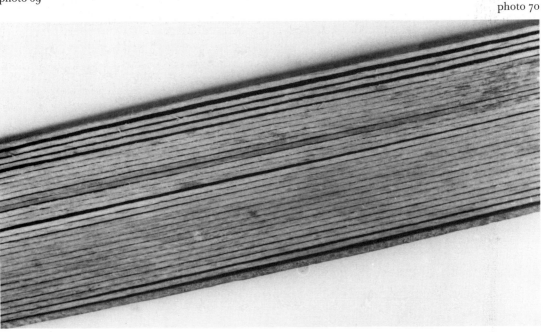

photo 71

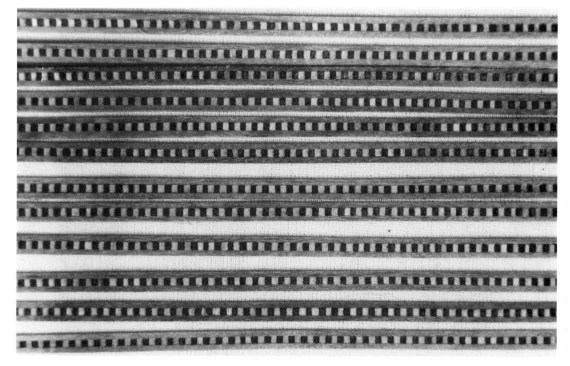

photo 72

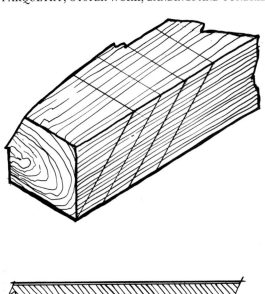

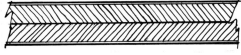

diagram 37

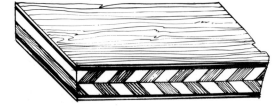

diagram 38

photo 72a

"Grand Panorama of the Great Exhibition", showing the Tunbridge Ware section, from The Illustrated London News 1851.

photo 73

Tunbridgeware

At one of my lectures someone once remarked on the patience of the people who individually created the tiny mosaics of wood called Tunbridgeware. The idea of people sitting down and actually doing this is mind-boggling. Tunbridgeware can be likened to bandings or a stick of Blackpool rock, with its name right through, cut across in slices. Royal Tunbridge Wells gave its name to this technique, and has a superb museum and exhibition of the work.

Tunbridge was a wood working centre from the earliest times. Late-seventeenth and eighteenth-century Tunbridge turnery was famous; painted furniture, penwork, and engraved prints used for decoration on furniture were just some of their techniques. However, the mosaic pictorial work must be the most famous. Names of some of the firms survive: Thomas Edmund, Barton & Nye, Henry Hollomsby, Robert Russell.

Their inclusion at the 1851 exhibition shows how popular the work was (photo 73). From the smallness of some of the objects, such as pencil cases, stamp boxes, card cases, pin cushions and, rulers, plus the popularity of Tunbridge Wells as a spa, it does carry all the signs of a souvenir and tourist-trade attraction. It was also much more than this, and survived as a technique for a long time – as a poster in the museum shows. This advertises in 1923 a Tunbridge tea caddy, looking for all the world like one from 1850, which was selling for 126 shillings – a formidable price for those days. Occasional tables with a full Tunbridgeware top depicting a square rigged ship were also on offer.

The work depends firstly on design, and since all the mosaics are of square or oblong fillets, these were made on graph paper; so in diagram 39 each square relates to the necessary wood strip carried in stock. For example, the dot might be boxwood and the X ebony. Using this graph the block was made up so that it can then be cut across the face to produce a man-made oyster. Should a customer have ordered one hundred boxes with a lid, the first task would have been to prepare the graph in the diagram. The block or blocks were then glued up, and when dry the man-made oysters sawn off.

The blocks were small, 100mm (4 in) to 150mm (6 in) long, ranging up to 200mm (8 in) maximum. The diversity of woods used was huge, 180 different species being stocked. The glueing problems must have been considerable; the larger blocks were produced from small sections glued together. Many glueings would have been necessary to achieve some of the quite amazing beauty and intricacy we can now enjoy.

65

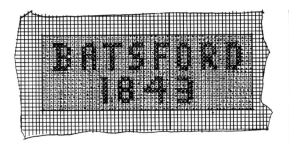

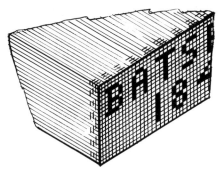

diagram 39

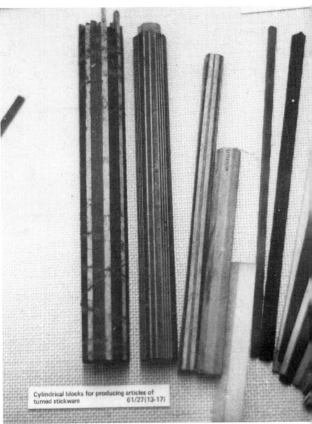

Cylindrical blocks for producing articles of
turned stickware   61/27(13-17)

photo 74

The work was usually small, and so depended greatly on accuracy. It is this factor in work often so small that I find intrigueing. Photo 74 shows blocks glued up for turned stickware. It needs little imagination to see how glaring any inaccuracy would be on the finished articles. Marks from the string which held it all together during drying are there to be seen, and show the basic simplicity of the process.

Earlier in the chapter we showed how a cubework surface was made up. In photo 75 blocks of similar pattern have been created to be sawn through and through, the surfaces used for card cases, small boxes, and the like. Photo 76 shows a cutting list for a graph, a selection of blocks and a veneer, sawn-off ready for laying.

The articles exhibited at Royal Tunbridge Wells are varied and cover the whole range of the technique, and the condition of the articles is superb. Since their condition is almost without exception original, it says much for the stability of materials and the glueing methods used, plus the understanding of the curators and the conditions in which the collection is kept.

The most amazing creation of all has to be the mosaic butterfly (colour plate (iii)). We are given its name – Vanessa Juliana – so the re-creation must be exact. Each area of colour is created with mosaic, the squares being less than 1mm ($\frac{1}{32}$ in) wide to create this work of art. Thirteen thousand individual pieces of mosaic were used. Edmund Nye was a master.

It is interesting to note that the old system of template sawing was used to inlay this butterfly into the boxwood ground veneer. An interesting sidelight to this subject is that Robert Russell of Tunbridge Wells developed a method of template cutting for marquetry to combine with Tunbridgeware, using ox-bone for templates to saw repetitive designs. The date for this is around 1850, and says much for the largeness of the world in those days, if we consider that totally accurate and repetitive stamping of wood and brass had almost

photo 75

photo 76

photo 77

photo 78

photo 79

run its span of popularity in London. A tiny industry could still stay within its boundaries and pursue its own developments.

The method of production of the stock for this work may be hard to understand until the small workshop is seen laid out. The date of this is from the last half of the nineteenth century (photo 77–8). The treadle circular saw carries an 8 in blade. The top of a small hand-driven circular saw can be seen in the bottom-left-hand corner. The bench in photo 78 has glued blocks, and on the bench tiny 3 in diameter saws from the hand circular lie about. Stone pots of heavy shellac varnish can be seen, and further down the bench are four blocks made up, ready to be put together and glued to make a finished floral pattern (photo 79). All that is missing is the dust and shavings, or the smell of glue in this little workshop that abounds with tools and examples of the trade.

However, it is no coincidence that the excessive use of bandings as a form of decoration began seriously about 1845 to 1865. Reproductions from this time and later were covered with bands of all shapes and sizes. Articles from one hundred years before were given the same treatment and inlaid with mass-produced decoration of shells, flower plaques and even small pieces of Tunbridgware. Bandings were put where no inlay bandings should be. However, as always we have one thing to fall back on – the frailty of human hands, and their inaccuracy when compared with machines. It was without doubt the early treadle and hand-driven saws that gave the extraordinary accuracy necessary for the production of Tunbridgeware.

—4—

Wood inlay: the technique

Those of us who wish to create a picture with the saw and knife may not feel up to the task without the facility of a fully-fitted workshop. These pictures at first glance appear to be almost an impossibility, but the methods, if the basic techniques are followed, are simple ones that will yield satisfying results.

If anyone does possess a cutter's donkey and is familiar with its use, then these instructions are not necessary. Many others will possess a small treadle fret, others a small throated jig-saw, some a vibro-saw (diagram 40), and thousands will possess a standard fretsaw and possibly the smaller piercing saw. Eclipse saws use the frame numbers FS70 for the former and PS50 for the latter. How nice to have such simple identification; FS; fretsaw, PS; piercing saw!

The saw blades for these come in various sizes. The wood-cutting variety are prefixed W, the finest, $W\frac{1}{10}$, has a blade dimension of width .011 in $\times$ .034 in depth and a saw pitch of 32, or 32 teeth per inch. They run upwards in size, prefixed W0, W1, W2, up to W6. W6 measures .22 in $\times$ .060 in with a tooth pitch of 16. A $W\frac{1}{10}$ will cut very fine scroll-work up to 4mm ($\frac{1}{4}$ in) thickness, but with care greater thicknesses can be satisfactorily cut. Other saws are available; one called Eberle Blitz is made in Germany, again the range starts with 0 as the finest and progresses through 1, 2 and so on for coarser blades. 0 is again excellent for fine scroll-work. These saws carry a very useful distinction; unlike the Eclipse, which have a square back, the Blitz's is slightly rounded, which will assist greatly in the turning of

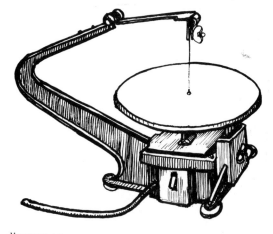

diagram 40

the saw during hand work, or turning the work if the saw is in a machine. Between machines, personal preference must be your guide, though they must be able to carry these fine saws or be adapted to do so. However, of all of them the vibro-saw, once mastered in use, has the tremendous advantage of not cutting you!

To the uninitiated the use of these hand fretsaws can be difficult. Since their cutting edge can be used vertically, horizontally, sideways or upside down, there is no limit to the number of cutting positions, which is only restricted by the user's physical limitations.

The frame-saw has changed very little since its invention. The steel frame of the saw gives the tension to the saw blade. The depth of throat is

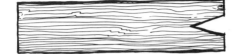

diagram 41

diagram 42

broken and tempers frayed, but, as with all things, with practice the knack will soon be found. Because of the vertical action and the delicacy of shape to be followed, a way of supporting the work is needed. The usual way, and I imagine the way from the beginning, is to make a support from a piece of flat wood with a V cut, as in diagram 41. The sawing is carried out in this area, two fingers usually hold the work down over the V cut-out, while the saw follows the pattern. These saws cut very fast indeed, and if this method of work is adopted – and it is the usual way – protect the middle finger from the possibility of a cut. Adhesive plaster is good, but personally I favour a light copper ring covering the vulnerable area of finger in front of the saw.

The actual sawing is not easy and I will not pretend that it is. Moving the saw up and down, and at the same time keeping it as vertical as possible, while following the pattern and moving the work, will take time and practice to master. The knack is to make the saw cut *slowly*. Turning the saw is another knack; the simplest way is to put slight back pressure on the saw while continuing the sawing motion, and then turn either the saw or the work. Practice will soon reveal all these problems; more practice will show just how precise and small the work is that can be achieved.

Before continuing, the division between sawn marquetry and knife-cut work must be discussed. In early inlay work the saw and knife worked together. When veneers were sawn, marquetry was sawn, and when the ability to knife-cut veneer began (and veneers cut accurately to about 0.5mm ($\frac{1}{50}$ in) or less became commonplace) knife-cut marquetry was introduced. I liken marquetry to drawing pictures with a saw; the incredible pictures achieved by the knife-cut method call to mind pictorial woodwork. Diagram 42 illustrates the idea; first shaping one piece of veneer (B in the diagram) overlaying it on to the next veneer (A) and cutting around the shape of B to transfer it to A. The principles are exactly the same as for the early intarsia. The cut around B must be gentle, initially just enough to break the surface fibres. Acute curves are marked by pricking; three, four or even more cuts are often necessary to cut satisfactorily through ven-

usually around 300mm (12 in), and since the saw is used vertically, the weight of the frame is put upon the wrist and the user needs to become accustomed to this. The depth of throat will govern the size of work, and constant re-threading of the saw through the work and re-tensioning of the frame must be mastered. Many blades will be

eer A. Soft, smooth and firm wooden beds are essential for satisfactory knife cutting.

The knives suitable for this work are many and varied. Craft knives by Stanley are good; I have used one design, No. 915281, which carries a good selection of blades. Scalpels, if obtainable, with their insertable blades, are excellent and do guarantee an immediate sharp edge. One problem is that as soon as the point of the knife is lost its cutting power is also lost. These knife blades are excellent but they are sharpened to a V edge which will produce a V cut. To achieve the perfection I have seen with knife marquetry, a knife with a half V edge would be required to produce a vertical cut. In the early days workshops did not like to incur the expense of throwaway blades, and used to make their own knives; a broken hacksaw was a useful source. The rake can be as fine as you require (diagram 43). When grinding do not *blue* the metal. Grind back one side to at least 4mm–5mm ($\frac{3}{16}$ in) and treat the resulting knife as a chisel; sharpen on an oil or whetstone as you would for that tool. The handle can be whatever suits you, wood with a saw-cut to hold the blade and bound up with string being one of the oldest. Soften the top of the blade with heat, insert this in a handle, drill through and use two small nuts and bolts let in flush to hold it. Or (the simplest method of all), make your blades to fit the craft knife handle of your choice. To be able to make the tools you require for a specific job is a very advantageous thing, and has been common practice among tradesmen since workshops began.

To elaborate a little further on the knife-cutting of pictorial woodwork, the use of overlaying of veneers is one way to achieve a chosen design. Another is to make up a specific part of the picture. For example, a house can be fully assembled, laid in its place on the ground veneer and cut into place; this is known as window cutting. The selection of veneers and colour contrasts can bring endless variety to the results. Small specific pieces of veneer can be selected and inlaid or windowed into place. A small-eyed piece from a burr or burl will create the most natural eye. Similarly, I have seen them used to create feathers so natural that it is difficult to believe a tree and not a bird has

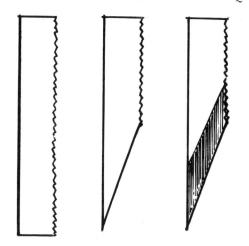

diagram 43

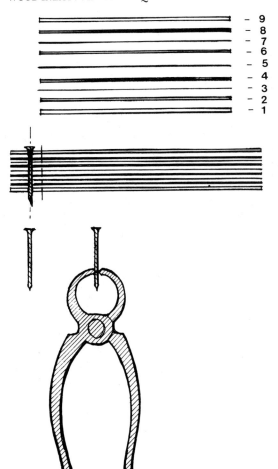

diagram 44

photo 80

grown them. As a tradesman I must confess to being amazed when confronted by the skill and artistry of these pictures. The technique of knife-cutting is well-supplied; kits of veneer with comprehensive instructions abound and have introduced countless people to the art.

Continued use of the sawing technique in the production of a design (assuming that a sufficiency of practice has produced confidence in its use), can employ many methods. The two principal and most simple ones will be explained here.

When a parcel of veneers was put together for use in the donkey, the method appears to have been to lay the veneers one on top of the other, nailing them together and putting them in the

donkey vise to saw through. However, it is a little more complicated than this in practice. The design shown in the drawing of the tulips from the dust pattern. To make a nailed and clenched parcel cut with the hand fret, such as would have been used in the donkey, use the method in diagram 44. Remember the nails that clench the parcel together must be outside the finished picture size (photo 80).

In the diagram the parcel is as follows:

1 A heavy waste veneer, or today a piece of 2mm plywood
2 Veneer for the ground (walnut)
3 In the early days a sheet of tallowed paper, today a sheet of wax paper

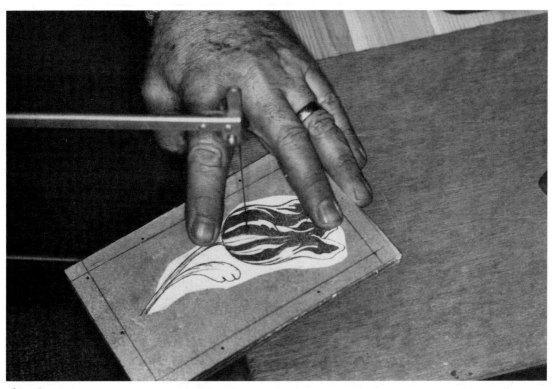

photo 81

4 Veneer for the stem and leaves (green sycamore)
5 As 3
6 Dark part of tulip (purpleheart)
7 As 3
8 Light part of tulip (boxwood)
9 As 1

One tip here: before driving in the nails or fine panel pins, nip the points off, your veneers will not split if this is done. Clench or bend the ends over, and remember to bend them into the area of your waste veneer.

This parcel is just under 9mm ($\frac{3}{8}$ in) in thickness. In the days of the donkey the jaws would hold the parcel together around the sawing area; the tallow paper helped to lubricate the saw. The wax paper today will stop vibration and you will not need to use so much hand pressure when the fretsaw starts to cut the shapes.

Before any sawing begins, the picture must be studied and the method of sawing determined. Remember that the veneers are only held together around the outside edge. Photo 81 shows the first cut and photo 82 the result. This cut begins from the fine hole drilled where the stem joins the tulip, at the right side of photo 80. The sequence of cutting follows, always sawing into the veneers that are held together (photos 83 and 84). The results of the sawing, and the numbered sequence of that sawing, is shown in photo 85. The next stage is to assemble the pieces; photo 86 shows this. In practice we produce four pictures in one sawing, each with a different colour combination and a different ground colour from the four veneers used. The fragility of the method can be clearly seen; to produce the tulip ten saw cuts are necessary. These work in such a way that when the tulip is fitted together the result is a flower smaller than the original drawing. These cuts produce a saw gap in the ground of at least 1mm ($\frac{1}{26}$ in) which is not acceptable (photo 87). The ground veneer was included in the parcel to illustrate this point. When sawn work is examined, this cannot be seen. More often than

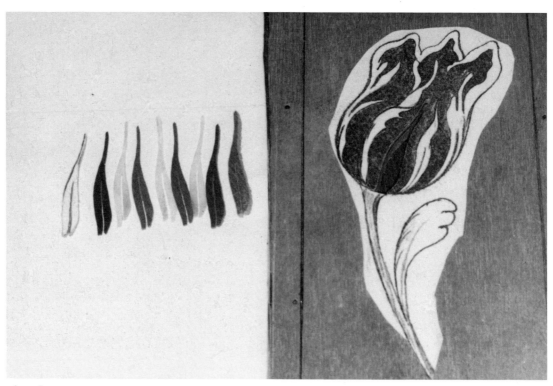

photo 82

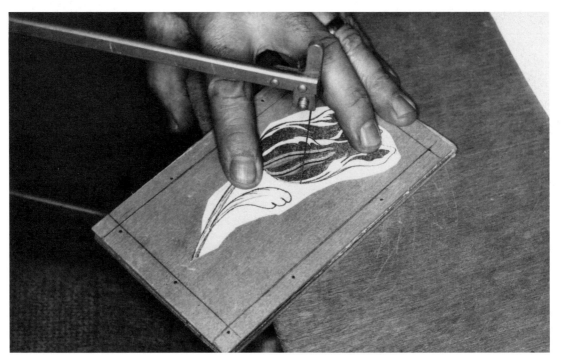

photo 83

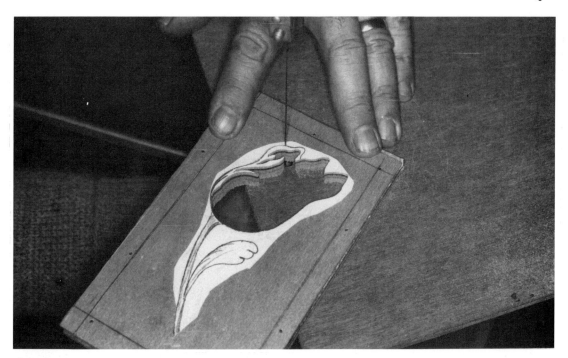

photo 84

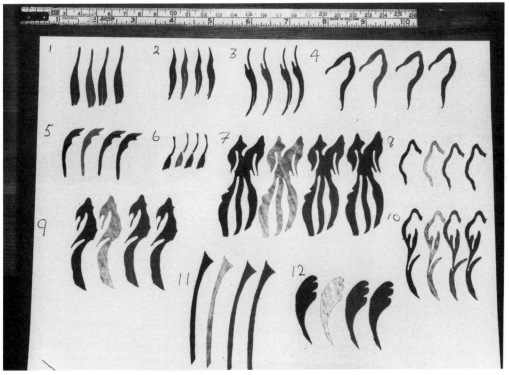

photo 85

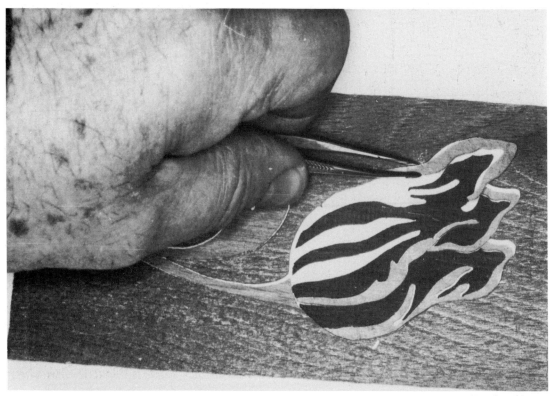

photo 86

photo 87

76

photo 88

not the work sawn into the ground shows a better fit than the marquetry itself. The solution is template sawing; the tulip and leaf being laid on to the ground, and this used as a pattern for the saw to cut it into place. In photo 87 this method has been used for the flower on the left; the right hand side is as it came from the parcel. It is sometimes said that a dovetailed or angled cut should be used to ensure a perfect fit, or even an angled table made up for this purpose, but this is not necessary and not advisable. If any angle is thought necessary it is the saw that must be angled. However, if this angled cut for template sawing is used it can cause an over tightness of join that will lead to problems when laying the marquetry.

I have found from experience that when sawing the work into place, a very slight angle away from the work occurs automatically; possibly because sawing follows the line where the article being sawn in place joins the veneer being sawn into. But more probably this is caused by an inbuilt

caution not to cut into the tulip! (photos 88, 89, 90).

The angled or dovetail cut needs further explanation. The problem is that there can be no constant angle to work with. If two modern veneers, 0.50mm ($\frac{1}{50}$ in), are to be dovetail-cut into each other – so that the top veneer becomes a perfect fit to the bottom – using a saw 0.100mm (0.008 in) thick the angle of cut is approximately 20°. If the thickness of veneers is enlarged and the same saw used (the usual practice) then this angle will lessen, until when carrying out the sawing of two veneers of 2.5mm ($\frac{1}{10}$ in) in thickness with the same saw the angle is about 3° and can be discounted.

I have never found dovetail sawing in marquetry work to be a common practice. The guides on a donkey are there to help, if not guarantee, a 90° cut through the work. To set them up with an accurate cutting angle would not be possible. The tilting bed of a vertical saw would be a different proposition and could be used. Dovetail sawing

photo 89

can only be used for two veneers and has its place in repair, usually in the world of brass inlay and boullework, when it can be used to advantage for holding down awkward areas.

The next phase is the production of repetition work. The parcel size of 100mm (4 in) × 160mm (6½ in) can easily be increased to accommodate four tulip flowers of identical pattern. The parcel is made up as diagram 44, but built up as follows:

1 Waste veneer
2 Box
3 Tallow paper
4 Purpleheart
5 Tallow paper
6 Box
7 Tallow paper
8 Purpleheart
9 Waste veneer and pattern

So with a slightly larger parcel, four tulip-head patterns can be laid on. One sawing would produce sixteen tulips. Similarly, for the stems and leaves a parcel of coloured sycamores can be made up; the patterns for the stems laid in one

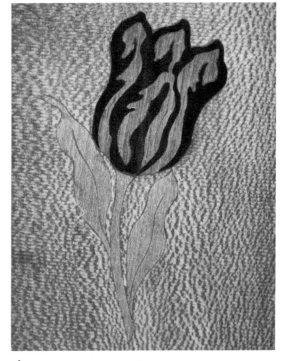

photo 90

direction of the veneer grain, the leaves in an-other. It was this system which created the extraordinary repetitive marquetry patterns of birds, insects, and floral work through the years, and was the only method before the advent of mass production for veneer and inlay in the last years of the eighteenth century.

When the small size of sawn marquetry is considered – or the fineness of a point that some work has been sawn into – with the fact that loss of these fine points is a common occurrence, an alternative way of holding the veneers must be considered. Photo 91 is the other tulip from our drawing – the parcel is made up as previously. However, in this case the top and bottom waste veneers are dispensed with; the wax or tallow paper is replaced by absorbent tissue or newspaper.

This process uses Scotch or animal glue weak-ened down to a strong size. The four veneers are size-glued together with the absorbent tissue or newspaper in the glue joints between the veneers. The parcel is put in a small press or under pressure until dry. Using such weak glue about thirty-six hours is necessary for this; cold hide-glue weak-ened down can also be used. No adhesives other than animal (hot or cold) are advised.

This parcel is only 4mm–5mm $\left(\frac{3}{16} \text{ in}\right)$ in thickness. A finer saw can be used, but before sawing begins tape the back veneer with a gummed paper, or glue on paper when the parcel has been made up. Use masking tape over the grain or include a waste veneer in the parcel (the traditional method); this waste veneer or paper have just one purpose – to stop the saw *ragging* or tearing the last veneer to be used in the actual work.

The advantage of this method will become apparent the moment sawing begins. The tulip can be sawn out immediately (photo 92), and a smaller saw frame can then be used to saw the pattern (photo 93). The whole flower becomes four pieces, and nothing falls apart. The only problem is to take it apart (photo 94). Moisture should normally be kept away from marquetry, so releasing the work might lead to problems of distortion. This is the reason for the paper and very thin glue. Animal glue at full strength has a

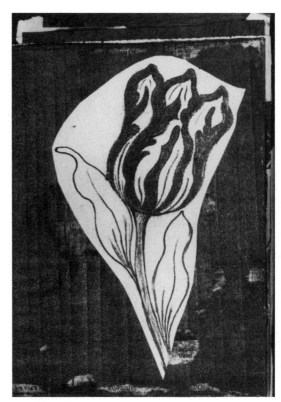

photo 91

low melting point. Halve its strength and its melting point is almost halved. A few seconds laid in steam and the whole parcel comes apart. Diagram 45 shows a simple way to achieve this.

When the pieces are parted, lay them on some paper with a flat board on top to prevent distortion. The four tulips in photo 95 were produced this way; the fineness of cut can be seen. The ability to saw to a fine point without damage or loss is a distinct advantage gained if this method is adopted. Photo 96 shows the tulips assembled; no distortion has occurred – and this is before they have been assembled and glued to the paper ground. This is an ideal method for produc-tion in quantity. Photos 97 and 98 show how the tulip-heads have been produced with a four-veneer glued parcel.

When the Petworth panels were restored (colour plate (v) and photos 99–103 are of new work necessary for the restoration), veneers had to be sawn to the necessary thickness. This was possible with the sabecu and box, but not with the

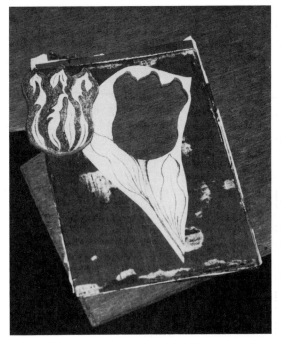

photo 92

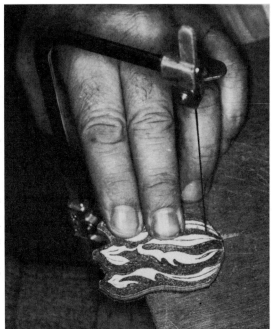

photo 93

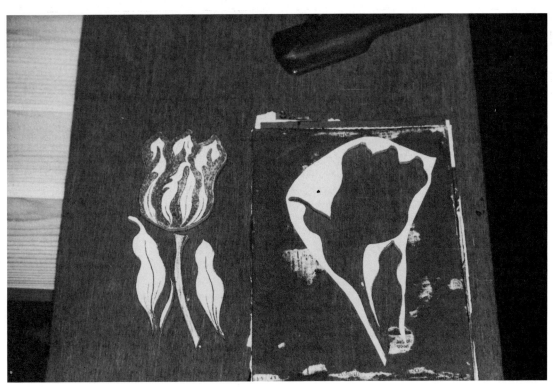

photo 94

diagram 45

dyed sycamore. It was necessary to glue four thicknesses of veneer to produce the $2\frac{1}{2}$mm–3mm ($\frac{3}{32}$in) thickness necessary. The method was to use a urea formaldehyde glue, in this case Cascamite, glueing the four veneers together to produce a plywood. This glue is ideal since it is non-staining, waterproof and to a degree heatproof.

The repair and restoration was long and complicated. Photos 99 and 100 are of two replacement doves, which were cut on a vibro saw. Three veneers were in the parcel and the glue size method used. These doves were large, 360mm ($14\frac{1}{2}$in) from head to tail. Strangely, the feet were not missing and are original! The bird in photo 101 is not so large, 105mm × 80mm ($4\frac{1}{4} \times 3\frac{1}{4}$in), and it contains 58 separate pieces when sawn. Photo 102 is the bird sawn before separation; the saw cuts down the wing area reduced the size by 3mm ($\frac{2}{16}$in). This was a three-veneer sawing and photo 103 shows the bird sawn into place on one panel. Had the ground veneer been included,

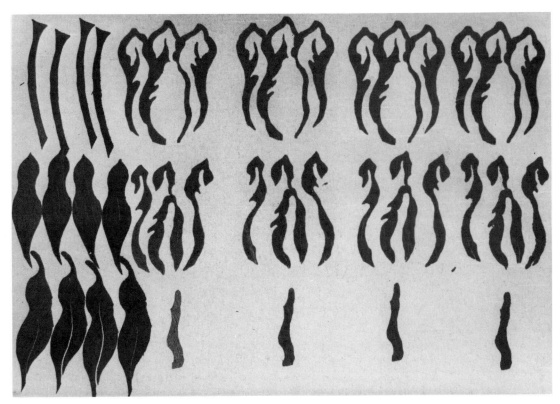

photo 95

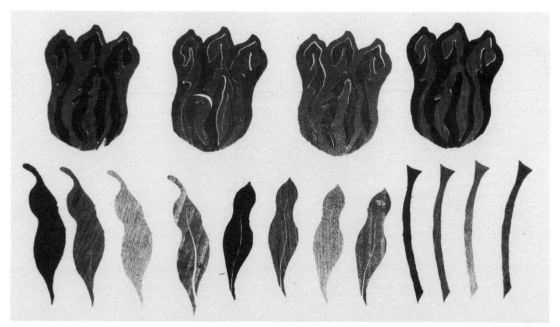

photo 96

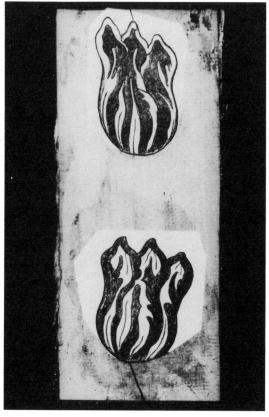

photo 97

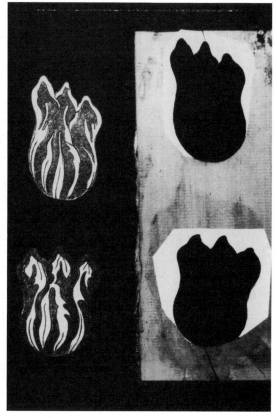

photo 98

photo 99

photo 100

photo 101

photo 102

photo 103

nothing like this sort of accuracy would have been achieved. The bird in photo 103 is the third bird produced by the sawing. It has been animated and glued on to newsprint to hold it together. It is during this process that the joins move together and the size of the object decreases.

Animation

This is the next stage after sawing. The sand tray, with its heat source, requires one or two accessories. The first is a pair of snipe-nose pliers; a pair of long tweezers is also useful, and something to smooth and shape the sand (I use a waste veneer). This becomes a good indicator of the sand's heat.

Toasting has already been illustrated. The delicacy of shading possible can be seen in photo 104; a section of fan is being shaded. The method should be to move the section forward; the heap of sand in front shows this. Photo 105 shows the result with one quick pass through the sand. The

animation of the lighter woods, especially boxwood, is far easier than the darker woods. Darker woods do not adapt as well, and caution should be exercised as charring can happen very easily.

Sometimes a shaded area in the middle of a piece is needed. Mark the area, and with a small spoon keep a continous heap of very hot sand in place (diagram 46). When long curves require regular shading (convex or concave), contour the sand into the shape of the piece; this makes control much easier. Toasting is a fascinating part of the process which has scope for continuous experimentation. There are more techniques to be tried than I have space to set down here. Always keep a small brush available to clean all the sand away; it tends to get everywhere. Finally, if you decide to thicken up all your veneers, which does make sawn work easier, remember to check that your glueing will stand the heat of the sand. It will pay to reduce the heat of the sand and use waste veneers to test what temperature is best.

photo 104

diagram 46

photo 105

photo 106

Assembly

If a marquetry surface has been made up and the ground veneer included in the cutting, the number of veneers used must be kept to a minimum, and the number of saw-cuts also (photo 106). Two is the most used in the marquetry, except in the acanthus flowers which were introduced after the ground was laid. One of these was missing, and evidence of the knife could be seen; photo 106 shows the area before repair. The replacement was introduced in the same way. During restoration much of the surface had to be lifted, and evidence was found of the sawing of ground and pattern together. This particular panel was very large and the sawing was more than probably cut on a vertical swing saw of a type much used in the late eighteenth century. The small pieces of green sycamore were introduced after laying, as were the acanthus flowers. They have retained their

photo 107

almost emerald green. The dyeing agent here was arsenic, causing a chemical change in the wood that does not fade. This plate also shows the use of sand-contouring to create the long and evenly shaded sweeps of the work.

If marquetry is symmetrical in its design, it will make little difference on which side it is laid. The procedure after sawing would be to undo the parcel, lay the ground on to a flat board and assemble the required pieces into place to create the picture. The problem is that it must be moved and handled. The solution is to glue the work lightly to a sheet of paper, fine linen, or anything that will successfully hold it together. Again, the adhesive must be an easily reversible glue. When all this is done and the surface dry, keep it under slight pressure between two boards (chipboard is ideal), until the time for laying arrives.

photo 108

photo 108a

The assembly will be different if the picture is asymmetrical. If the forgoing applies, and the ground is included, remember to assemble it reversed. The paper must be glued to the finished or uppermost surface of the picture.

When template sawing is to be used, each item of the surface should be animated and assembled on to its paper. Again, each must for convenience be reversed; it is important to have a copy of the design in reverse to assemble. If the original is on tracing paper, a reverse copy can be taken by photo-copier, or by tracing on to a sheet of paper behind which is a reversed carbon paper.

Now glue the individual pieces to the pattern. The saw joints will all move together and become quite tight. When all is dry the flower, bird, or other design can be handled; it can be surprising just how strong it will have become. In the days when ready-cut surfaces to veneer or inlay into place could be bought, they were prepared in this way. Often with antique work the paper was not removed. Dates can sometimes be found, as can places of origin, as far apart as Dublin and The Hague.

The size of throat carried by the saw will always govern the size of picture, unless the ground veneer is arranged in such a way that it is the same size as the throat of the saw. Feathering is one answer (photo 107) – the small doors are mirror pattern marquetry, the top is not – but the method is awkward. One half down the centre feather is cut first and the floral work down that line removed and laid on the other quarter; this is then sawn in. A stem below the escutcheon hides the join. The evidence can be seen; on the bottom doors the feather line of the ground is straight, but on the fall it does not follow a straight line – a rare sight. A huge amount of marquetry is created by making the individual pieces, laying the ground and then using the earlier techniques of intarsia to cut them all into place; this has been used on the top of the item in photo 108.

Laying

This method of marquetry, combining the saw and knife, must be discussed and illustrated. Many times I have seen articles condemned as being inlaid later; usually this applies to articles that are veneered. Obviously, fashion, price, and

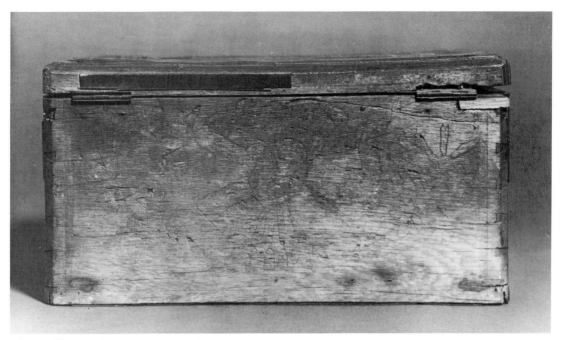

photo 108b

photo 108c

commercial gain has decreed that it should be done and the results will not deceive the experienced. However, it was a common practice in the world of small marquetry and I am fortunate to be able to illustrate this technique. The origin of the box (photo 108a) is German, *c.*1770–1780, decorated in the classical style of the time. The ground veneer is sycamore, an ideal wood for the knife in intarsia. As can be seen, the condition of the box is poor, its size being 320mm (12½ in) × 215mm (8½ in) × 165mm (6½ in). The work is professional and the surfaces original. Photo 108b shows the back. By some extraordinary quirk all the back veneers have been lost; on the oak ground the surface picture can be seen. This mark was left by the knife as the ground veneer was cut through. Some remnants of the back had been saved, and were left inside the box; photo 108c shows the top right-hand corner. A small piece of sycamore with its leaf decoration still in place was one of these remnants; the overcut of the inlayer's knife can be seen, and the engraving is well executed.

Our next illustration, photo 108d, shows the back of this veneer. The joins are tight and not sawn. It can also be seen that the toothing does not marry up, as is usual with a conventional marquetry panel. Here we are looking at the technique of cutting out all the shapes with the saw, then overcutting them into the ground veneer after it has been laid. Photo 108e is the flower from illustration 108c shown on its edge. The sawing can be seen, and the fact that a small angle has been introduced purposely which accounts for the excellent joints you see on the surface of this form of work. It is in this type of work that dovetail sawing is used; this is the only time I have seen positive evidence of it.

The last illustration, photo 108f, is the ground veneer. No saw marks are evident, but at the point above and to the left of the thumbnail you can see where the knife has failed to cut right through. Compare this point to the appropriate place on photo 108b and you will see there that the groundwork does not carry the tell-tale mark of the knife.

The quality of work on this German toilet box is amazing, and is evidence of a technique rarely

photo 108d

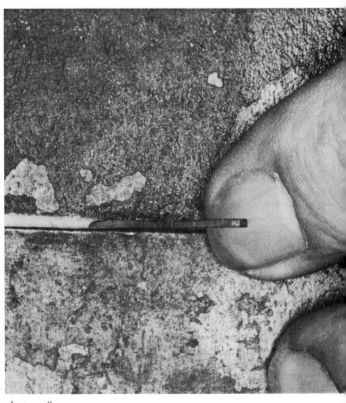

photo 108e

93

photo 108f

used. Yet the finest intarsia workers emanated from its place of origin, Southern Germany. They would obviously have used the techniques that they knew best and these would almost certainly be the traditional ones.

To lay a picture needs an adhesive. The list available today is huge, but until the end of the nineteenth century and probably until after World War II, hot or cold animal glue was all that was ever used. Today, we have a bewildering selection. Super glue adheres in seconds. Evodes cover both surfaces with a thin film; they should be allowed to dry and then put into contact for an instant bond to occur. Urea formaldehyde (Cascamite), simple to mix and use, will not cause discoloration, and is waterproof and heatproof to a large degree. Araldite epoxy resins, if the correct temperatures are followed, can be used to glue aeroplanes together. One- and two-part resin glues are totally waterproof, and will withstand continuous boiling and temperatures so low that the wood itself will fracture first. PVA (Polyvinyl

acetate), a white adhesive for wood, is a familiar product. This list is a small selection of what is available, and yet no glue has the vital property of hot and cold animal glue; none are easily reversible. Simple reversibility in the glueing is in some instances essential; this consideration applies mainly to antiques. Moreover, after laying the veneer, to discover a mistake or movement and be unable to make a correction can be an intolerable frustration. This cuts down the list of adhesives effectively to hot and cold animal glue or PVA.

There are three methods of laying, as follows:

1 Lay the picture from one side and build and glue each piece into place as you move across.
2 Lay the ground veneer and then with intarsia cut the pieces into place.
3 The traditional and without doubt the most satisfactory way: lay the whole surface, held together with its paper or linen, in one operation.

This can be treated under four headings:

1 The ground
2 Preparation of the veneer
3 A simple press
4 Time and method

1 The ground

As we know, this is all-important, and must carry no flaws of any kind. It can be plywood; a minimum thickness of 9mm ($\frac{3}{8}$ in) is recommended and if the picture is over 300mm (12 in) square it should be thicker. Blockboard is good and should be of the best quality, with a double veneer finish over the cores. Chipboard can be used and solid wood is fine as long as it is clean, stable, and carries a clamp across the grain at each end. Any knots or faults must be rectified before laying, or photo 109 will be the result.

2 Preparation of the veneer

When the surface is turned over, the chances of all the veneers of the glueing surface being of the same thickness is not very great. The method used to flatten the surface is known as toothing. This is now archaic, and the chances of finding a toother are remote, but a good substitute is shown in

photo 109

diagram 47. A piece of fine hacksaw blade becomes the toothing iron, and the short handle is useful to hold it with. Use it very gently in all directions and the results will be excellent. It will do no harm to start on the ground first, which will give the feel of this improvised toother, if it has not been used before.

3 A simple press
This can be made up; diagram 48 shows what is probably the easiest. I do not possess any form of veneer press, and all laying of decorated surfaces and heavy veneers has been carried out using this system. A typical workshop lash-up which is entirely satisfactory is shown in photo 110.

1 Bearers; these are usually 50mm (2 in) or 75mm × 50mm (3 in × 2 in), the former are usually more than adequate; they need to be about 150mm (6 in) wider than the actual boards of the press.
2 A piece of chipboard or blockboard about 25mm (1 in) larger all round than the surface being laid.

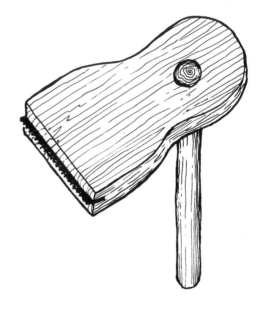

diagram 47

3 The ground.

4 The veneer, marquetry or parquetry panel.

5 A sheet of thin polythene.

6 Ten to twelve sheets of newsprint.

7 The caul. This is again a piece of chipboard or blockboard of the same size as no. 2.

8 The top bearers, the same dimension as no. 1.
Plane one surface to a curve with a drop each end of about 5mm ($\frac{3}{16}$ in); the reason for this is that at each end of these bearers the clamps start the pressure. Because of the curve the pressure begins at the centre and moves outward. The cramps or clamps will need to have about 150mm (6 in) centres, so for a 300mm (12 in) square press six will be needed; these can be hired if they are not part of your equipment. Another way is to use coachbolts of a sufficient length and drill the bearers accordingly in the overhanging part.

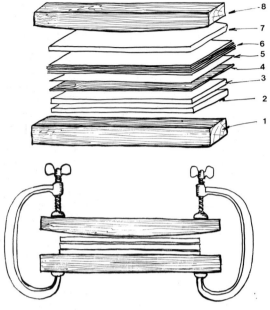

diagram 48

photo 110

i Top of table from the Gobelins Manufactory, Paris,   ii Enlargement of plate (i)
   c.1680. (Courtesy J. Paul Getty Museum)

iii Butterfly Vanessa Juliana, made by Edmund Nye. (Courtesy Royal Tunbridge Wells Museum)

iv Interior of small desk, German, attributed to Anton Lautenschein, *c*.1700. (Courtesy Detroit Institute of Arts)

v (Opposite). Modern three-part cutting of parrot, technique of overcutting with knife for replacement. (Private collection)

4 Time and method

Time is usually not on your side! Because of this, set the whole press up and make sure it works. Get into the habit of doing this, and then take it all down, remembering where each piece is for ease of re-assembly.

Whichever glue is used, follow the directions. With some the time factor is limited, and with Cascamite the curing begins immediately the glue is mixed. If a contact glue is used, spreading each surface evenly is vital, as well as accurate positioning of the veneer on the ground. Personally I would not recommend a contact glue, but they can be used and the press will help hugely in their success. With PVA you will have limited time. After *both* the ground and veneer have been covered, assemble as quickly as possible – but do not rush. Cold hide glues are very much like PVAs. They have one disadvantage; a limited shelf life.

I have used all these glues successfully except the contacts. These have only been used for laying plastic laminate and to veneer copper, brass and aluminium in modern work. My personal preference is for hot animal or scotch glue. Because heat is what makes it stick, time is on your side. Heat can be re-introduced as required and this means complete control of the timing; by varying the heat the glue is always quickly and easily reversible.

Scotch glue will probably be the only one that does not carry explicit instructions on its preparation. When in its two-part steamer a simple test for readiness is to lift a brushful of glue upward. When the stream of glue breaks into drops, the brush should be about 150mm (6 in) above the surface. The glue can be thickened or thinned with water until this consistency is achieved.

Using Scotch glue, glue the ground and then the veneer. Do not rush; the trick of successful laying is to let the work cool down, and then assemble everything. Lay the veneer on the ground and fix it in its correct position; two or three fine pins will usually suffice. Leave about 1mm ($\frac{1}{24}$ in), with the heads clipped off, standing proud from the surface. Lay on the polythene and paper. The vital part is no. 8, the *caul*. This is now heated up; the easiest way is a blow lamp. It needs

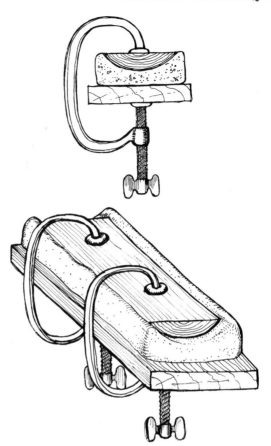

diagram 49

to be heated all over its surface to a temperature just too hot to touch. Lay it heat side down on the paper and put on the bearers and clamps. Tighten these down evenly from the centre outwards. Do *not* tighten fully; allow the heat to do its work. Three to four tightenings over a period of ten to fifteen minutes are ideal, and then a final twist forty minutes later.

The heat retention is astounding and cooling will take up to two hours. The amount of glue pressed out is surprising. Leave the work for at least 24 hours; the reason for the polythene will by then have become obvious. At this stage, wash off the paper, re-assemble and allow to dry for another 24 hours, or as long as you can give it. The beauty of the system is that if you wish the caul can be re-heated, which will greatly assist the drying-out.

Shaped surfaces present different problems. Sandbags were used to push veneers into shaped grounds and are totally satisfactory today. A good canvas bag, 100mm (4 in) larger than the area to be laid, is two-thirds filled with silver sand. This is heated and laid on a firm surface, or a heavy board the size of the bag. The work is glued and held in place on the shaped surface. Lay some paper on the sandbag and cramp the shaped surface down. The bag will follow the shapes perfectly and hold everthing in place (diagram 49). If cold glues are used, the heat can be dispensed with and the method will still be satisfactory.

For some shaped work the use of fibreglass or GRP (glass reinforced plastics) has great possibilities for making accurate glueing moulds. Remember to allow for the veneer thickness when taking your mould from the shaped surface. Heat cannot be used with GRP, but if 3mm ($\frac{1}{8}$ in) thick rubber on top of the veneer is also allowed for when making the mould, this can be used for heat conduction. This is a very satisfactory way to exploit the advantages of animal glues. The reason for my continued harping back to the use of the most old-fashioned glue in this era of miracle adhesives is that you are always in control, and the results are reversible; a vital point if problems develop in the laying of shaped work.

It is not within the compass of this book to go into the making of GRP moulds. Excellent literature on the subject is available and will supply the information far better than I can. Explicit instructions are supplied with the materials.

All being well, the panel of work is on to its ground. It is advisable to veneer the back of the ground to the same thickness as the front. Therefore, if a knife-cut surface is laid, cover the back with a veneer of knife-cut thickness. If a thickened and sawn surface is laid, use a thickened veneer. It has always astounded me that veneer was always used on one side only. Working with old surfaces one sees the huge warping and distortion problems caused by one-sided veneering. It is incredible that it was over 250 years before compensating veneers became a normal pattern of work. This says much for the cost and complexity

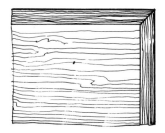

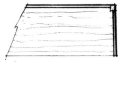

diagram 50

of veneering in the early days.

The panel or picture when laid will benefit from an edge decoration. The methods are many and varied and diagram 50 shows only a few. The advantage of a reversible glue will now become apparent. It will be necessary to cut back the edge of the picture or remove the veneer if an edge decoration is required.

It is always easier to put an edge decoration on after the surface is laid. This can involve a crossband or long-grain veneer in a contrasting wood, or the same wood as used for the ground veneer. If the edge of the surface is to be seen, remember to veneer this edge first and lay the surface veneer over that. The cutting-in of a long-grain square of wood around the edge became common practice in the late eighteenth century, and this is a good and decorative way of keeping the edge veneers of the surface from being damaged.

The cleaning-up of a decorated surface can be difficult. Heat must be kept to a minimum. A good old-fashioned scraper is without doubt the best initial way, followed by glass paper of various grades, finishing with the finest of flour paper. Be cautious if machine sanders are used. They can remove timber very rapidly, as well as causing heat and its attendant problems. When the surface is finally sanded, wipe over with a clean cloth and clean water. When dry, the surface will feel rough. Lightly sand smooth and the surface will not roughen again when polishing begins.

Many people ask what happens to the saw-cuts. On cleaning up with glass paper they will fill with dust. This will coagulate with the glue from the small amount of heat generated, and all this makes an excellent filler.

Finishing is up to the individual. My own preference is to seal with two or three coats of a good transparent shellac polish, rub down with flour paper between coats and finish with a good wax polish. The softness of this finish is best; a glossy finish will have the same effect as glass over an oil painting.

Restoration

The difference between old colour and new colour must be understood. The faded and all-over golden colour that a panel of marquetry with any age at all bears, has no relationship whatsoever to the article when new. The problem for the repairer is that the difference between the old colour of the veneer and the new colour is miniscule; between five to eight thousands of an inch being the division. Usually the old surface colour is maintained – and for reasons of antiquity and value it must always be kept. The surface may possibly be engraved: to abraid it to bring back colour will ensure that this engraving is lost. Furthermore, on much work the engraving will in fact be penwork; abraid it and this will also be lost, so caution is advised. A detailed examination

of the surface is the first priority.

If the surface dates from before 1780 to 1800 and is original, it will almost certainly have the problem of 'lipping'; i.e. a lifting around the sawn joints of the marquetry. This is a natural phenomenon and will usually appear parallel to the grain of the veneer. It will usually be accompanied by a series of cracks along this grain. If this effect is minimal then leave well alone. If it is severe and there is no veneer loss, the problem should be tackled with care.

The reason for this 'lipping' is almost always glue failure and the thickness of veneer used. Glues eventually dry out totally, and with marquetry and the many open joints or saw cuts on the surface this will always happen far more quickly than with a normal veneer. With old work it will be necessary to use animal glue. However, before re-laying of the 'lipping' can begin, check for dirt and dust. A very fine piece of brass shim metal cut to a fine strip can often be inserted and will enable most of the dust to be loosened and blown out. Then wash the area over with warm water. Do not be too liberal. Dry it off, then wash over with a 50% solution of hot animal glue. Wash well in, wipe off the surplus, and cover with some absorbent paper; paper towels are ideal.

Set the whole panel up as for laying a new one, but include a sheet of hardboard or masonite. This goes between the newspaper and caul. Heat this instead of the caul, and assemble as described. Two, or sometimes three heatings may be necessary, but the method will usually be successful and will solve all but the very worst of the 'lipping' problem. Severe examples, usually caused by far too much dirt under the surface, will necessitate the removal of the whole piece of veneer. Often a whole area may have to be lifted. The recommended way to lift a veneer is with hot water, using a hot iron and a wet cloth to steam it off. The rule is *never* lift a veneer with water and steam if you want to preserve it and its colour (or re-lay it).

Cescinsky (in *The Gentle Art of Faking Furniture*) states 'soak a cloth in linseed oil and use a hot iron over this'. This will certainly remove a veneer, but it will also totally change the surface colour. A sure and safe way is to cover the surface with masking tape (not sellotape). This is not necessary but it is a good idea until the method is familiar. Photos 111 to 115 show the process. Shave some beeswax on to the surface and with a hot iron melt it over the area to be lifted. Keeping the wax just above melting-point, metal shims can be slid under the veneer as the glue melts and then rapidly dries. To be able to remove a piece of marquetry without it falling apart is a very useful knack. Keep the base of the iron smooth, making sure no burrs mar the edges. Modern electric flatirons are excellent for this purpose; the ability to have an accurate temperature control is a great advantage. I use an old fashioned flatiron since it is all that was available to a certain James Little when he was young.

James Little was a tradesman whose apprenticeship began in 1882. His reason for using the flatiron was that beeswax was used to polish with, often hot, 'and that never did any harm, did it?' He was right. It will never discolour a surface or distort the veneer. When used with care the flatiron will not even cause problems to a polished surface. I often wonder who James learned this from.

Other reasons for veneer removal include severe warping, rot and the one most often found, our old and inevitable friend the furniture beetle. Truly severe cases of the last have but one solution; to cut the ground away from the veneer. The same applies to rot (photo 116). In the case of severe warping, run the panel over the top of a circular saw to within 3mm ($\frac{1}{8}$ in) of the veneer (photo 117), or take the ground away with a router until 2mm–3mm ($\frac{3}{32}$ in) of the ground remains. Using this will make it pliable enough to re-lay the panel with 2mm of ground on to a new and unwarped surface. Often, however, the 2mm of ground left is of such a rogue character that it will pull the new ground out of shape and must be removed completely. Cover the veneer surface with masking tape, or glue paper or fine linen to it. Hold it down on a flat board and with a paring chisel cut the last 2mm–3mm ($\frac{3}{32}$ in) of the ground away from the veneer. Photo 118 shows this; already the banding of the panel can be seen.

Think of the surface as a painting. The canvas is always removed from the paint, never the paint

photo 111

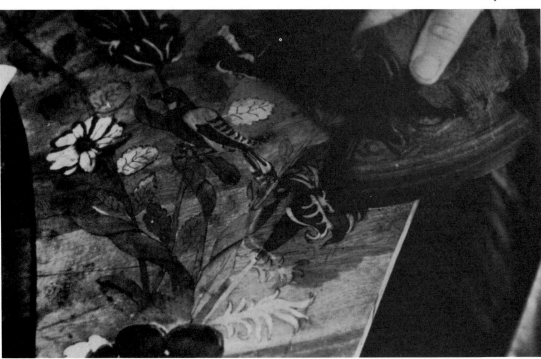

photo 112

photo 113

photo 114

photo 115

photo 116

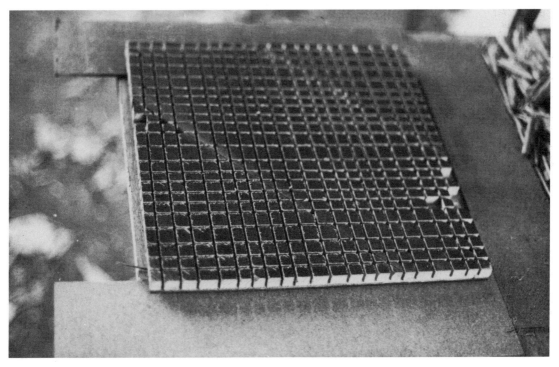

photo 117

photo 118

photo 119

from its canvas or panel. By using this method no distortion will occur, and the veneer will be a firm and stable material to re-lay. Photo 119 shows a surface after a rotted ground has been removed. The veneer is from the late seventeenth century and shows the toothing preparation, and even faint evidence of the sawing in the top right-hand area.

To repair and replace a piece of old marquetry can be difficult. Sometimes it is hard to identify the wood. If the surface is anywhere near original, it could well be very much thicker than any which will be carried in stock. A method of thickening up the chosen piece for repair will have to be used. Obviously, if it is possible to have the wood in the solid, it is far better to do as was done in the beginning and saw your own veneer to near the necessary thickness, then prepare it in the normal way.

Assume that a flower is missing, or partly missing. Before any repair is attempted, make a good and fair copy of the missing article. Drawing, tracing or a rubbing can be used (diagram 51). I prefer the latter if the whole flower is missing; it is often possible to see the shape still on the groundwork. If this is not the case then the character of the missing piece can almost always be found by study of the remaining work.

The chances of copying the original to fit exactly are slim. My own method is to make the replacement piece slightly larger than is needed, and then revert to the knife and inlay techniques to ensure a good (and to all appearances sawn) fit. The parrot (colour plate (v)) when made up was replaced using this method. After the replacement has been made, ways and means of cleaning up the surface should be found; the replacement surface is best finished before it is put in place. By reducing the thickness before it is finally glued in place the fit can be made almost exact, and it is therefore possible to create the correct colour in the repair before the work is even laid. This is a good habit to get into and will solve the many problems of flushing-down and complicated colouring after the laying has been done. This system must be used when it is essential that the old colour of the marquetry be maintained. If this is not necessary, and re-finishing and bringing

diagram 51

back to a newer colour are wanted, then normal marquetry techniques can be applied.

Odd though it may seem, the majority of marquetry repair is not the replacement of loss, but repair of cracks and splits in the groundwork. Unhappily, most groundwork was not made to live in the world of modern heating, and simply from the nature of the grounds used, cracking will abound. Pulling a crack together is never really possible. The wood has taken up the position it wants to be in, and it is prudent to make sure that it is now secured in that position.

The first problem is that the surface around the crack will not be level, and methods of holding the face level must be found. Flat bearers can be cramped across the crack. Sheets of newspaper either side of the split can be used as adjusters to bring the surface level up. When this is achieved, and it is possible with most surfaces, some way of holding it in this position is needed. From the back, fit a fillet of the ground wood very accurately indeed to the depth of the face veneer, and glue with urea formaldehyde. When fully cured the face surface can be restored; leaves made larger to cover the crack, small areas of ground veneer accurately put in place. It is astounding how these ugly splits can, with care and patience, be lost cosmetically. When this work is undertaken, a golden rule is not to leave the article out of its usual habitat and conditions for one moment longer than is absolutely necessary. If it is remotely possible, try to re-create the conditions of normal habitat during repair.

It is a continual effort to re-create the correct temperature and humidity that particular articles came from. To look for a stable set of figures for a set of circumstances applying to a time about which we know very little, is an approach I find difficult to understand. Even when articles are kept in stable conditions the movements will still go on. Wood and adhesives are natural things; our unnatural conditions often seem to be death to them. However, I believe that humidity is more important than temperature, and if a temperature range between $58° - 65°$ F can be maintained, coupled with a humidity range of 48% to 55%, then movement may be kept to a minimum.

It appears that we can only make-do and mend. To expect articles made 200 or 300 years ago, created from air-dried materials with glues dependant on humidity, to survive in our modern world is asking a lot. Continuous repair, restoration, and then conservation is necessary. However, the way man-made laminates and boards, veneered using modern adhesives, do stand up to the conditions of modern living proves the point; crafts still change to fit the times.

— 5

Metal and repetition inlay

Brass inlay or brass marquetry preceded boulle-work by many years. What is the difference? Simply answered, it is that the former involves brass inlaid into solid wood or sawn into a veneer, whilst in the latter, brass has wood inlaid or sawn into it. This is speaking from the point of view of the workshop and tradesman; it is often the practice to call all brass inlay boullework, regardless of the materials used. Obviously, a piece of furniture veneered with ebony and brass, and attributed to the workshops of Andre Charles Boulle, must be considered as *boulle*.

Fine wire is probably the earliest form of metal inlay; wires of gold, silver, copper, brass, and other metals were inlaid into a groundwork of solid wood, in patterned forms. However, brass is by far the predominant metal used for decorative surfaces, with pewter running a poor second. It was the unique alloying properties of brass that brought this about, as well as the ability of lacquers to make it appear almost like gold.

Photo 120 is from a piece that dates from *c*1750, and uses brass and ebony, with a brass ground form. It is of interest to examine such as these and make comparisons with work cut into ebony veneer grounds of around one hundred years earlier. The crudity of the earlier cutting shows up to a startling degree, as well as the obvious problems encountered with the sawing of metals. We can be sure of this, since it must be assumed that the men producing these surfaces would be fully skilled and at the top of their trade.

The 'two-for-the-price-of-one' sawing idea used for the tulips in chapter 4 can also be employed with brass inlay work. Photos 121 and 122 show this technique clearly. This bracket from the early nineteenth century has been veneered on one side with brass inlaid with ebony. The brass outfall was then inlaid into ebony and used to veneer the other side. Similarly, the legs shown in photo 123 are from a split-top desk of the latter part of the seventeenth century, and again show the idea to perfection; although in this case three materials were used: pewter, brass and ebony. To veneer the legs thirty two faces were needed. Repetition work has always been an important process in the production of the decorated surface. The two marquetry panels (photo 123) are a classic example of a design and its ground produced with one sawing. Photo 124 shows the front of this desk.

The pattern and development of the work is similar to that of marquetry. Metal inlay first flourished on the Continent, yet its appearance was slow in the British Isles. It first showed itself with simple inlay lines, often of pewter combined with ebony. The work was mainly in the style known as 'seaweed', or very fine scroll marquetry. At this time fine quality bureaux and bureau bookcases veneered with 'mulberry', and inlaid with these scroll patterns made of pewter, began to make their appearance.

Photo 125 is a side fret from a bracket clock of 1750. The job was to replace a fret that was missing; the existing original fret is on the left, which had been sawn from a single veneer. Workshop practice is to saw these single veneers on a sheet of pewter – or today, aluminium. Metal,

photo 120

photo 121

photo 122

having no grain, is the ideal material to hold the delicate veneer up against the pull of the saw. The end result can be clearly seen, the metal forming the backing from the new fret after it was sawn. This very old method could have been used for 'seaweed' marquetry; the outfalls from the pewter used could be the reason behind the fine inlaid pewter scrollwork that suddenly appeared, and just as quickly vanished.

The ground veneers for brass inlay are norm-ally from the hard exotics; ebony, kingwood and rosewood. Their toughness holds up well against the hardness of the brass. It is a surprise when the brass inlay work of John Channon (whose work can be seen in the Victoria & Albert Museum) appears in the middle of the eighteenth century. His superb brass cutting, and even more superb engraving, was inlaid into veneers of mahogany – and often into solid mahogany. He does appear to have been unique in this form of decorating

photo 123

photo 124

photo 125

surfaces, until brass inlaid work became popular at the very end of the eighteenth century. But at this date inlays are almost always found to be pierced into exotic hardwoods, rosewood and kingwood being predominant, with rosewood having by far the major share.

It was the neo-classical revival leading into the nineteenth century that produced an era of rosewood furniture, beautifully inlaid with hand-cut brass, and engraved on the finer pieces. Chairs of beech were grained to simulate rosewood, their cresting rails veneered with rosewood which had intricate brass patterns sawn and laid into them as a panel of marquetry. Chairs and lounging furniture were constructed from solid rosewood veneered with brass inlay patterns. Circular breakfast tables were often made in pairs in which the one- and two-part cutting methods could be exploited. There was an explosion of work in the new fashion. The workshops of Bullock and McLane became famous. Boxes in every shape and form

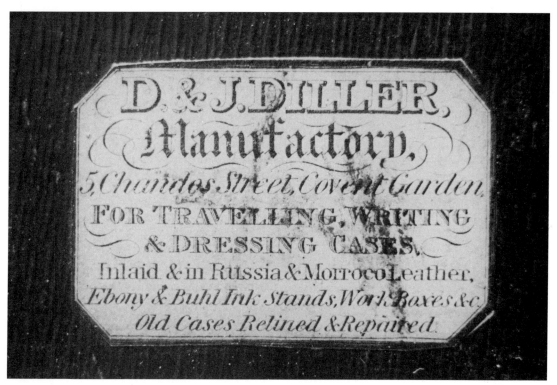

photo 126

appeared, and one such maker working in 1805, employed a trade card with the English spelling of *Buhl* appearing (photo 126). So it was that the period from 1790 to 1850 created the styles of rosewood and brass inlaid furniture. The Royal Pavilion at Brighton, Sussex, displays many examples of this technique in what is probably its most elaborate form.

Another name to come on to the scene around 1800 was that of Thomas Hope. He was not a cabinet maker, nor a designer in the true sense of the word. From the workshop and tradesman's point of view, Hope was a perfectionist; the frailties of human hands had no place in his approach. On the subject of metal inlay techniques he writes 'At Paris they have been carried to a great degree of elegance and perfection. The metal ornament, and the ground of stained wood in which it is inserted, being, there, stamped together, and cut out, through dint of the same single *mechanical* process, they are always sure of

fitting each other to the greatest degree of nicety.' (*Household Furniture and Interior Decoration* by Thomas Hope, (1807)).

In Paris the architect and designer Jean Percier was using this repetition inlay system. At the end of the eighteenth century craftsmen in the British Isles were introducing it to an unprecedented degree. The initial work would have been wood to wood and explains the incredible repetition inlays of honeysuckle, tudor rose, pimpernel flowers and circular fans created with an accuracy beyond the scope of any techniques used before.

The accuracy was such that there is no room for a saw or knife; the join of the inlay to its ground veneer cannot be seen (photos 127, 128, 129). When this work has been removed and held to a light source, no light can be seen to come through. This work always stays in excellent condition. The cause of damage in the past, the saw cut, has been done away with, so the joins all over the decorated surface are dispensed with and failure

photo 127

photo 128

photo 129

around these joins cannot occur. The surfaces, whether of wood marquetry or of wood and brass, survive, often in their original condition.

Examination of articles will demonstrate this. One problem complete accuracy produces, more prevalent on the wood to wood surface, is the occurrence of stress fractures on the ground veneers. Examination will show the fine hair-like cracks along the grain direction. These can be seen in the illustration. The cause is twofold; the tightness of join and the impact of the stamp – the impact being quite an impressive sight.

Photo 130 is of a mahogany ground wood and photo 131 shows the veneer just as it was removed. Covered with glue it is not very distinct. Judging from the mark on the mahogany, the pressure is far more on one side than the other. Note that the veneer of photo 131 has been turned over; this pressure can be seen on the veneer. The side or edge of this veneer can be illustrated, (photo 132); it is a full millimetre ($\frac{1}{32}$ in) in thickness, and no evidence of sawing can be seen. The most impressive examples of this technique – which led to mass production twenty five years or more before the industrial revolution – must be the rosewood

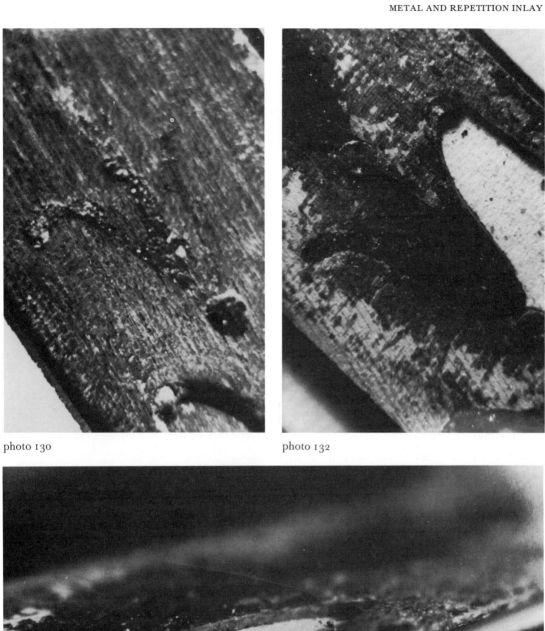

photo 130

photo 132

photo 131

photo 133

photo 134

and brass inlaid furniture. Photo 133 shows a small area of the top of a writing box by Messrs. Diller of Chandos Street. They did not have the facility of stamping; hand-sawing with its inaccuracies, the saw-cut with its glue line and the usual failure point can be seen in this example of English *Buhl*. We are probably looking at work from the end of an era. The reading-table in photo 134 is covered with totally accurate stamped brass, even to the degree that the outfalls from the frieze have been inlaid into the plinth and the column. This example shows that stamps can be used separately and the work not necessarily stamped together.

In this small table the sheer quantity of inlays is remarkable, remembering it is only 530mm (21 in) × 460mm (18 in) and 700mm (30 in) in height. The list of stamped inlays:

Greek key	6.6m (21 ft 6 in)
Strip triangle inlay	12.6m (41 ft)
Frieze	1.8m (6 ft)
Outfalls from frieze	3.0m (10 ft 6 in)
Brackets on plinth and top of column	16 in all.

The quality of this small table is extraordinary. During repair it was necessary to replace about 150mm (6 in) of Greek key. This was the only significant damage, on the sides at the top. The top itself was in perfect condition. To saw this repair work by hand took four hours; to have cut all the key would have represented 172 hours

photo 135

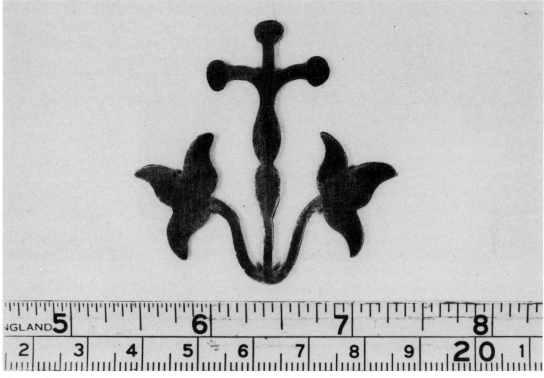

photo 136

labour! On this assumption, to hand-pierce the whole table would have taken five hundred hours.

To have created these surfaces by hand-sawing, the labour costs would have been astronomic. Since selling prices for these articles survive, we can ascertain that this mass production method allowed that work to come within the purse of many consumers, until the usual outcome of more and more, cheaper and cheaper became the method's downfall.

The technique of buying in ready-made work had existed for a long time. Photo 135 shows a cross-stamping: we are looking at the back and the pressure of the stamp can be seen as a rounding over of the edge. A standard and common inlay is shown in photo 136; the back shows great rounding from pressure. The copper content in brass used for this form of inlay is much larger than the normal alloying; a zinc content of only 15%–20% is not uncommon.

The candle-slide from the reading table shown in photo 137 is made of solid rosewood and inlaid with triangle punchwork. Again with this the loss is across the grain; the frailty of wood and its continual movement is the cause. Look for the groove across the grain: laying in this groove is a strip of cedar mahogany. When these inlay strips were manufactured, the whole strip with its inlays was toothed and glued to a veneer of cedar mahogany which held it all together. The whole

photo 137

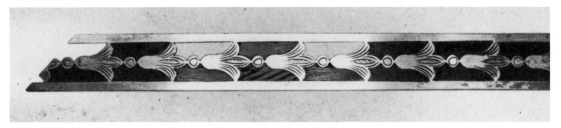

photo 138

photo 139

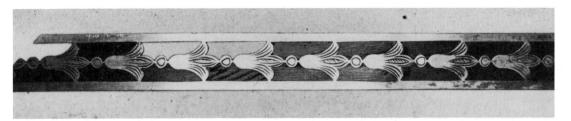

photo 140

photo 141

photo 142

assembly then inlaid directly into the article. The frailties of man as opposed to machine show up here. The work is original, and one piece of inlay has been put in with the triangle the wrong way round.

This small strip of inlay (photo 138) from a table made in 1804 illustrates the complete accuracy achieved. The sample is French and is of the finest quality, as the engraving shows. The ebony piece removed has come from the space directly below (photo 139). It has been moved one more space away from the mitre and replaced (photo 140). Finally, the piece of ebony beneath has been removed, turned over and placed in the metal, two places up from the mitre (photo 141).

The technique of laying on a ground veneer can be seen in photo 142. Only the metal is prepared or scratched up and the accuracy of the work can be seen. Photo 143 shows the edge of the metal, as does photo 132, with no sign of the saw, or of the burring-out that will always occur when this has been used. This small piece of material, only 13mm ($\frac{1}{2}$ in) wide and 140mm ($5\frac{1}{2}$ in) long, is from my bits and pieces collected over the years. It never ceases to amaze me. The table it came from had over 30 metres inlaid into it; this small piece I replaced, but my hands could in no way re-create the total accuracy shown in these illustrations. I have always found it hard to understand how the metal was managed with the wood (ebony is

photo 143

brittle) and how it was possible to stamp the four thousand pieces of ebony for this table without losing any of the points in the long grain – the points lost in the illustration were caused by my handling. As a technical and mechanical exercise it is amazing, and one which used the ability to create tiny repetition work at a price many people could afford.

Photo 144 comes from Paris. It is veneered inside with tulipwood, and the brass is stamped into ebony between kingwood. The accuracy is total; the ends are cross-banded with kingwood and inlaid with brass lines $\frac{1}{2}$mm ($\frac{1}{48}$ in) wide; a quadrant of brass shim is used to finish the corner. Yet it is only 180mm (7 in) wide. The feet and tiny lifting handles on the sides are gilded. The cost today can only be imagined; then only 25 shillings! This type of work eventually came to be taken totally for granted, and its popularity was comparatively short-lived. The reasons for this are many; changes in fashion, over-production leading to cheapness and with this, poor quality,

photo 144

and the sheer quantity that was inlaid – inlays often being stamped in with almost no thought for design at all. Couple this with total mechanical accuracy and the work can often become boring; so unlike metal inlay's exuberant cousin, boullework.

6

Boullework

In the early days the problems of veneering with wood were many; for anyone involved in restoration work the evidence is there to be seen. To devise a system of veneering with brass, pewter, copper, cowhorn, tortoiseshell, ivory and pearl must have presented the innovators with enormous problems.

The first problem to be considered is the completely different properties that the materials possess. They must all be veneered on to wood which shrinks with heat and will expand with dampness and cold. Metals expand with heat and shrink with cold, whilst animal products will generally remain unaffected. Surfaces put together with a mixture of these materials should not in theory stand any chance of survival, and many have only done so with almost continual repair, restoration and conservation.

André Charles Boulle (1642–1732) invented the technique. The longevity of the man was extraordinary for the time, but nowhere near so extraordinary as the longevity of the technique that bears his name. The production of boullework has never really ceased. It continued through the eighteenth and nineteenth centuries, when it was practised throughout Europe, and it is still possible to purchase articles that employ the technique today, although happily plastic often replaces the use of tortoiseshell.

The name of Charles Boulle has become synonymous with this type of work and though it is fair to say that he perfected the idea, he certainly did not invent it. It appears to have evolved in Italy, perhaps in medieval times, the use of copper and the Greenback turtle from the Mediterranean being combined to form a means of decoration in architectural forms. The walls of a monastery room are on record as being veneered in this way with copper and shell. But boullework is usually associated with France and the reign of Louis XIV: this is the place to begin when attempting to describe the craft. The development of a new technique must have a reason: the royal splendour of these times welcomed the creation of something that appeared to be veneered with gold or silver and inlaid with brilliantly-coloured designs.

The problems of the work must have been tremendous. The success of it depends very much upon the skills of the engraver. Some of the finest work is exquisite; for example the earliest work attributed to Piérre Golle and dated between 1675 and 1680. Sometimes a ground of pewter is inlaid with brass and red tortoiseshell. Referring back to colour plate (ii), we have marquetry and boullework successfully combined. A red shell centre is inlaid with brass and pewter. Pewter stringwork outlines this to combine with a *Guilloches* band of pewter inlaid with cowhorn, originally pale blue, now faded to grey. Each corner template is cut with an overpiercing of an acanthus leaf in brass, beautifully engraved. It is surprising that at this date (1690), the metals and shell are engraved, and yet 70 years were to pass before engraving was used on woods in marquetry. The rigidity of the guilds is well known and one must wonder if this could have been the reason.

photo 145

photo 146

vi Commode c.1710. Brass inlaid with under-painted
horn. (Private collection)

vii *(left)* Picquet table
attributed to Piérre Golle
c 1683. (Courtesy of the
J. Paul Getty Museum)

viii *(right)* Interior of the
flap from colour plate
(vii). The dolphins and
fleur-de-lis at this date
indicate royal usage

In fact, colour plate (vi) shows boullework at its most flamboyant. In this case the article, c1710, is totally veneered with brass and inlaid with coloured cowhorn, the colouring going far beyond a single shade for the flowers. Superb paintings on vellum are inlaid and have the protective cover of cleared cowhorn glued over them. Looking at an article such as this, it takes little imagination to appreciate the vast amount of work needed to saw out all the shapes and inlay them with coloured horn. It is because of this that the system of one and two-part boulle became a common practice. This is known as *première partie* and *contre partie* or *boulle* and *contre boulle*. Once again the material for a pair was almost automatically produced, and we have the history of marquetry repeating itself.

Photos 145 and 146 show how this was put to good use. The drawers from a pair of commodes show the technique, and it can be seen that in the first picture the brass inlaid into the tortoiseshell ground is in fact the brass or *outfall* metal that was produced when the shape was cut from the sheet brass of the commode in our second picture.

The commodes are known as a pair in one- and two-part *boulle*. The cutting will begin by producing the surface for the second commode. As with all decorated surfaces the first necessity must be a design, and some of these original engravings survive. Before a design could be of any use, the metal for the groundwork had to be manufactured. Sheets were cast, and then hand-beaten to the sizes required. Examination of the surfaces will show that the size of metal used was not over-large and evidence of this beating or blanishing, and then the toothing of the underside, can be seen on examination of early work (photo 147) – before rollers helped with the preparation of metals in later years. The underside has been prepared by the more familiar scratchings. Photo 148 again shows early work, though the engraved scratchings are later, probably when a repair or re-laying was carried out.

Before any work can start the design must be transferred accurately to the surface of the metal. The top surface would have been fully prepared – that is cleaned up, filed, or scraped to a finish – before the design was transferred. If this practice

photo 147

was adopted it would have been possible to engrave the top completely before any cutting began. This would explain the superb accuracy of the engraving; mistakes by the engraver on to the surrounding areas never seem to occur. The outfalls often show evidence of filing to straighten up a sawn edge, obviously where the saw has not followed the design accurately enough. Again, a bold, engraved line would without doubt have made the saw-piercer's job a far easier one. Photos 149 and 150 show this process; the brass is being held in a small vise. As it is only about 0.75mm ($\frac{1}{32}$in) thick, the sawing can be seen on the right as well as filing to straighten up the cut, which is clearly evident where the sawing marks have disappeared.

If the craftsmen creating boullework three hundred years ago had had our facility of accurate sheet brass or pewter, pre-engraving would have been a practical proposition. The amazingly accurate repetition of design that can be seen had to make use of known and practical techniques for copying. The technique of copper-plate etching has been known and practised for centuries. Since this required a fully-finished and burnished sheet

photo 48

photo 149

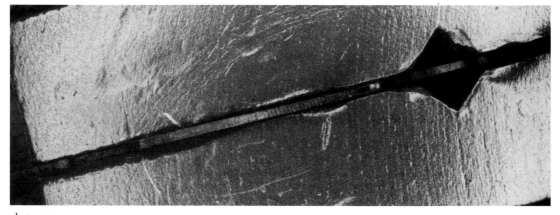

photo 150

of copper, it must follow that a sheet of brass or pewter could also be used and could be etched in acid by the same techniques. The etching could then be engraved before the top was pierced for boullework. Since we are in the realm of metalwork, of which the work of the horologist forms one area, the production of a fully-engraved surface before cutting must have been a possibility, since it is such a practical technique.

One aspect of this practicality is in the diversity of materials that can be used. When a surface of brass inlaid with shell or horn has been laid, the surface would have to be flushed down and prepared for polishing. It would not make sense to bring the hardest material, the metal, down to the softer shell, horn or wood. The surface would be set up so that the softer materials could be taken down to the metals for finishing, and a final burnish.

A second point is that when these surfaces are taken apart for repair, evidence of fine burring at the sawn joins of the metal would be expected.

This is normal when softer metals are subjected to even mild abrasion. If a surface was laid without any pre-finishing, or was laid with the metals thicker than the inlaid materials, then abrasion to render the materials level would be necessary.

photo 151

photo 152

photo 153

Evidence of this is hard to find. It is perhaps strange that no metal dust is found mixed in with the glue of the sawn lines that form the decoration.

Photo 151 is of a pewter panel inlaid with black rosewood. The engraving in the centre does look a little incongruous. To pierce this engraved shape would have made the work much easier. In photo 152 the starting-point for the sawing can be seen; the fine holes. The accuracy of the work here is outstanding. Admittedly it is pewter, which is easier to work, but the extraordinary likeness between the engraving in the centre when related to the inlays surrounding it must be considered in the context of the possibilities of pre-engraving.

This is workshop practice today, and the commonsense of the tradesman does not usually change. This pre-finishing can be illustrated: photo 153 is of a Boulle bracket clock from 1720. The view is from the side; no evidence of finishing can be seen after the brass was laid. From the case construction this can be a firm assumption. Under magnification no evidence of finishing *in situ* could be found. During restoration the metal was removed for cleaning since this was the only satisfactory way to clean into the corners, so to finish and buff the metal *in situ* would have been impractical. The curved area of the base was laid first. The sides, when fitted, were used to hold the base into position, a method used extensively when veneering surfaces with metal.

Metal is only one of the materials that needs preparation before it can be used in this process. The next most common material is tortoiseshell. It is always referred to as this – although it is in fact the shell of the turtle, the favoured species being the Hawksbill and Greenback. In seventeenth- and eighteenth-century France, a turtle was regarded as a fish, and to veneer a surface with fish skin would not have been acceptable: despite the fact that a much sought-after surface was shagreen or sharkskin. Hunted for the flesh as well as the uses that the shell could be put to, it would be fair to liken tortoiseshell to an early form of plastic; that is to say a material that can be malleable and worked into intricate shapes that will be retained. Everyone has seen the boxes and shaped backs of brushes and quite extraordinary diversity of other artifacts created by its use.

The animal, especially the Greenback, can reach quite large proportions, and the plates of the carapace are also large. Photo 154 shows a plate, or to give it its correct name a *scute*. This one is about 330mm (13 in) × 230mm (9 in), from an animal weighing about 48 kilos (110 lb). The carapace carries thirteen of these scutes, four down each side and five over the top, running from head to tail. The illustration also shows another part of the animal, the belly. This has a pale yellowish colour and can be used to advantage in repair work. The best shell was considered to be the Hawksbill or Cayman shell, which has been hunted avidly. Although now protected, its rapid decline continues.

The Hawksbill shell was known as the 'blonde' and can be recognized from its almost sparkling clarity. Hawksbill was always used on the finest work. The Greenback shell can often be very thick; up to 5mm ($\frac{1}{4}$ in) in places not being unusual. The Hawksbill is usually much thinner and far easier to prepare and because of this was allegedly removed while the animal was alive.

To make these shells of any use for boullework, they have to be flattened and thinned. The flattening is achieved by boiling in salt water and placing under pressure. The Greenback scute is usually thick and needs to be reduced to somewhere near the same thickness as the inlay metal.

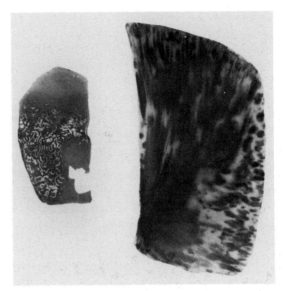

photo 154

Scraping was the usual way of achieving this; a long and arduous process requiring considerable skill. Today, it is still an arduous task, but helped considerably by the use of power sanders. However, hand scraping still produces the best finish for the shell's preparation, and it is advisable to continue with it anyway after the machines have done their work. The scraping of the Hawksbill will be far easier – scraping to clean up the surfaces is often all that is necessary.

The diversity of colours created in the shell seems to cause confusion. It is created by colouring the adhesive, which is achieved by mounting the shell on good white rag paper and using whatever colour is required in the glue. This adhesive would be animal or hide glue, with vermillion (mercuric sulphide) or sometimes red lead added for colouring. Lapiz lazuli would be used for the blue, usually on the finest work, and lead or zinc white for the pale amber effect; this sometimes has gold powders mixed in to produce a metallic lustre. The natural shell so often favoured is produced by umbers mixed with the glue, and paper sometimes being excluded.

No firm rules surround the use of paper and coloured glue. The paper is often omitted. It can be roughly divided up by nationality and date. Paper and adhesive was predominantly used on French and English work, coloured adhesive usually only in German (the drawer fronts in colour plate (iv)). From the practical point of view I would always use paper. The wood of the groundwork can never be seen when it is used. However, no matter what the nationality or century of the work, one fact does emerge; on the finest work the use of paper has always been in evidence.

The loss of shell from the surfaces when paper has been used nearly always seems to happen because of the failure of the paper; very rarely because of failure between the glue and the shell. This does prove the old adage of the compatability of materials. Animal glue to animal shell really does have a tremendous life and holding power: damage and loss to boullework is almost always confined to the metal part of the surface.

These are two main constituents of the surface; another metal used is pewter, and to a much lesser degree copper, though the latter can be treated in much the same way as brass. Pewter, an alloy of lead and tin, is always malleable and has a very low melting point; it must be treated with caution. When old it can suffer from a problem called 'pewter rot', a breakdown of the alloy that comes from the under-surface upward, a difficult and often tragic problem. The causes of this do not seem to be fully understood. One reason given is that when veneered to oak the tannic acid of the wood causes the decay, but this does not explain why pewter rot occurs when the groundwork is pine, a timber with carries tannic acid to a far lesser degree. It is also baffling that some pewters are attacked and some not when both are the same age and veneered on to oak. Pewter from about 1850 onwards never seems to suffer from this problem. From this time the alloy started to be controlled, lead being recognized for the poisonous substance which it is. Since we know little of the early methods and purity of the pewter alloys in boullework, it has always been my opinion that pewter rot could possibly be caused by the alloy itself. Odd things do happen to these early metal surfaces; brass often appears exactly like copper, and on cleaning is discovered to be brass, or 'yellow copper' as it was called in the 1700s. The phenomenon was caused by the atmosphere the article had stood in for many years. Zinc can leach out of brass, to such a degree that the metal is almost on the point of collapse. Whenever this is found, the environment is always near or on the coast; what salt water will do to brass is common knowledge.

As brass is the predominant metal with pewter second and copper a distant third, among non-metal inlays cowhorn is second to tortoiseshell, a material of great practical use for musical horns, drinking vessels or the sides of lanterns or lanthorns – and again an early form of plastic which with heat can be formed and hold its shape.

In modern days, with cattle de-horned, it becomes difficult to find a supply of what was once such a common material. The horn I use is imported from India. After the solid portion of the top is cut off, the remainder is cut down one side, and with heat and a lot of pressure, can be flattened. Photo 155 shows horn in this condition; as can be seen, it is neither transparent nor thin. The preparation of horn is difficult: first, a sight of a cross section will show that it can be cleaved, which is a great help in thinning it down for use. The plate of horn shown on the left is raw before any preparation, the plate on the right has been cleaved and the upper half of it is now about 1mm–1.5mm ($\frac{1}{16}$ in) in thickness. This cleaving can be done gradually and the horn stripped back, layer by layer, to arrive at a more manageable thickness.

It is rare indeed to find an area of horn that is naturally clear. Usually it is cloudy and white and a method of clearing the horn must be found. The traditional way is to use heat from an iron press with tallow or animal fat which drives the discolouration out. Photo 156 show this process, the piece of horn being about 300mm (12 in) long and 130mm (5 in) wide. Its left side is just as it came from the animal; the remainder has been cleaved or peeled back, scraped and sand-papered up. The last 80mm (3 in) has been covered with tallow and pressed between two blocks of steel heated to about 200°C. The cloudiness in the horn has been driven out, and the surface buffed and polished on both sides. Glued beneath is a small piece of shell to show its clarity. Photo 157 is an enlargement from the top of the colour plate (iv); the paintings on vellum can be seen. These brilliant miniatures were usually painted in tempera. The transparent horn was then glued over them for protection in exactly the same way as shown in photo 156. Photo 158 shows prepared horn backed with modern vellum paper; the shapes used were for repair to the illustrated Boulle commode. Photo 159 shows prepared horn. The glue, squeezed out by the press when the paper was applied, can be clearly seen, in this instance to produce some brilliant yellow inlay work. A word of warning; this is a very unpleasant and often smelly job. The thought of a workshop from the Guild of Horners in the early seventeenth century makes me shudder. It is possible to prepare large areas of horn this way, but I am sure that the difficulties would have been great. Articles veneered totally with horn are rare when compared with items inlaid with it.

It was the practice in the early days, when creating a *boulle* and *contre boulle* pair, to inlay the outfalls into a ground of natural tortoiseshell, then to inlay the brass sheet with these brilliant paintings covered with transparent horn. The startling effect created by this needs no further description. I have only seen one true pair of commodes created this way – the engraving on the brass outfalls identical to the paintings under their protective coverings of horn.

photo 155

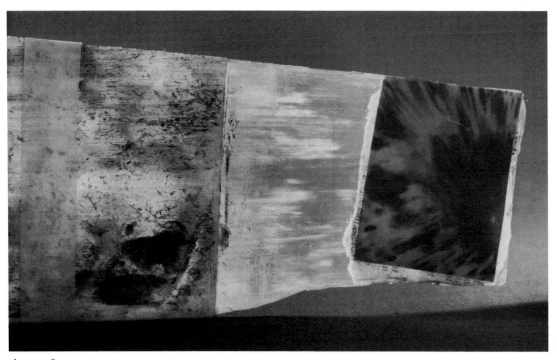

photo 156

photo 157

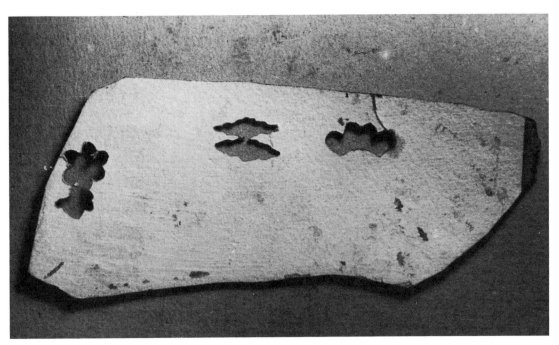

photo 158

photo 159

Ivory

The use of ivory has been so widespread it is a wonder any animals remain. It is a miraculous material that will carve and turn exquisitely, which can be pierced to an accuracy and delicacy given to almost no other living material. It will carry engraving, can be dyed and is a fitting material to have found its way into the decorated surface. It must be remembered that ivory is a tooth, and when sawn to a veneer it loses its enamel protection. The veneer will be pure dentine – this is quite soft and must be treated with respect. One of the major problems is to flatten it. Steam, or our faithful press can be tried. Another way is to soak the ivory in a weak 5% solution of phosphoric acid that will soften the material enough to flatten it; and enable it to be formed into simple curves and shapes. Never use a solution stronger than 5%; total disintegration can occur. Happily most of the problems with ivory in the decorated surface can be solved by the correct use of moisture and heat.

Ivory is often dyed green. Paradine is one dye used, as mentioned. It is highly poisonous and difficult to obtain. Aniline dyes are also satisfactory, the porosity of the material being a great advantage. A small piece of ivory soaked in the coloured spirit of an aniline dye for 24 to 36 hours will usually take up the colour required.

As has been said, the green dyeing of ivory and bone was very much a seventeenth-century practice and was used extensively for leaf-work in early floral patterns. It appears to have been gradually superseded by the ability to dye woods; the use of dyed ivory had almost disappeared by the early eighteenth century.

Ivory has its varieties. African ivory is larger and tends to yellow, carrying a coarser grain. Indian and Siamese are smaller, with a much denser grain, far whiter in colour. It was often the practice to whiten the glue before laying ivory, or to use clear fish-glue containing whitening; the purpose being to stop discolouration showing through the material.

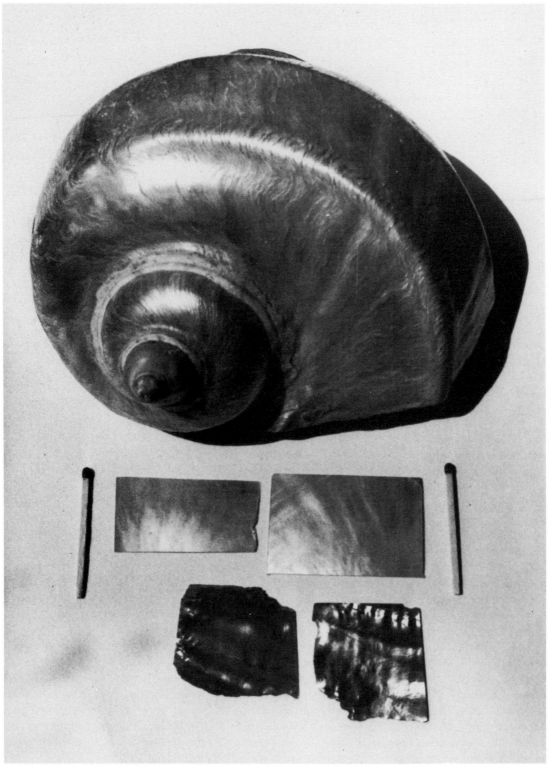

photo 160

photo 161

A final word of caution. With ivory, bear in mind the extraordinary way that modern plastics can copy natural materials. They can look, feel and weigh identical, and they can be almost impossible to tell from the real article. However, a red hot pin-point will usually disappear into plastic, but will not harm ivory.

Pearl

Pearl used as a form of inlay in boullework is really the 'odd man out'. It does occur and could be used

perhaps in a face, or an animal such as a cockerel or insect. Of all the materials it is the most intractable, as it must be sawn from the mother-of-pearl shell. A piece of pearl 75mm × 50mm (3 in × 2 in) would be a very large piece indeed, and this will affect the design of any work using the material, such as photos 160 and 161. The shape of the shell is here used to the advantage of the maker. It is non-malleable, cannot be softened, and is very brittle and hard. Because of this, the engraving will often appear crude and the edges of the engraving flaked. However, even with these

photo 162

photo 163

problems the popularity of pearl has not waned. The use of highly-coloured pearl from the abalone and other molluscs became a popular feature in much nineteenth-century work.

Saw Piercing

The ability to pierce metal in the most intricate way existed in many forms when boullework first began. The techniques actually used often seem to be enigmatic. It is stated that the method of sandwich-cutting wood marquetry was employed, except that the materials were glued together. This is hard to believe, since from the diverse nature of the materials used, the problems this could cause would be considerable. Surfaces with up to three different materials and five different colours are commonplace, requiring a sandwich of eight layers, and this would surely be totally impractical.

If we refer to the two commodes of photos 145 and 146, it can be seen that it would be possible to cut the surfaces by the sandwich method. However, when the commode of colour plate (vi) is considered, this method would be impossible and another system becomes necessary.

When the design is on the sheet of brass, the first task is to saw around the design completely. Photo 162 shows an area of a top that has been repaired, a brass ground inlaid with coloured horn. From the nature of the work an outfall of brass will result, as shown in photo 163. This can now be used as a template and the technique of template sawing used to inlay into a shell ground.

The top of the brass and horn inlaid commode (colour plate vi) must have been made using this method. This would be the only way that the painted inlays could have been created. It would have been impossible to create these by using the sandwich method. It is sometimes suggested that the sandwich work can be separated by water. This is difficult to understand when the presence of the coloured shell is taken into account; the glue and colouring on to paper would dissolve. It could not be sawn in its natural state, with coloured glue and paper applied after the sawing, as this would be impractical and time consuming. When boullework is taken apart, no evidence of

this can be found. What *is* found however, is that the sawing of the brass and its inlay do not follow each other. The brass shows the slow sawing we would associate with metal; the shell shows a much faster sawing and suggests that they were not sawn at the same time.

This can be illustrated. The evidence of the problems when the metal was being sawn can be seen. Photos 164 and 165 are from the early

photo 164

photo 165

photo 166

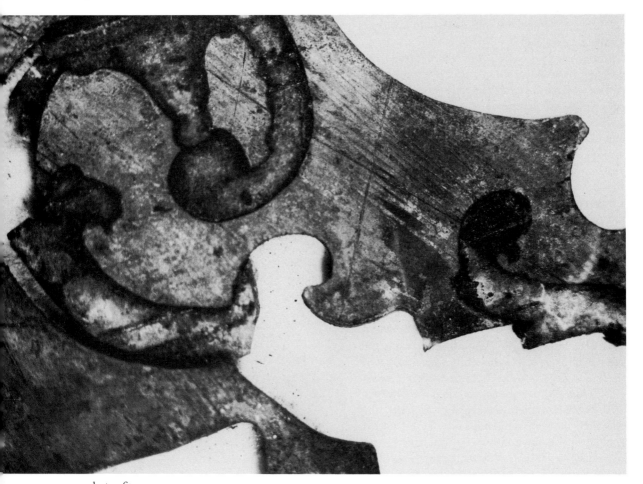

photo 167

photo 168

eighteenth century, and the sawing is freehand (not vertical) and very slow. Photo 166 is from a little later and cut in brass; without any doubt a vertical swing-saw has been used to create this form of saw mark. Photo 167 is from the back of a small piece of *boulle* from *c.*1710. The back preparation can be seen, the fine toothing of the metal and the burring from the saw. The darker areas are tortoiseshell, still with some vellum adhering. It is also possible to see that the shell was prepared before sawing; no toothing of the brass runs over the shell or paper. From the same source, photo 168 again shows the toothing, and the magnification is such that the burr from the saw is very evident. This burring is always to be seen, and again shows that after sawing and

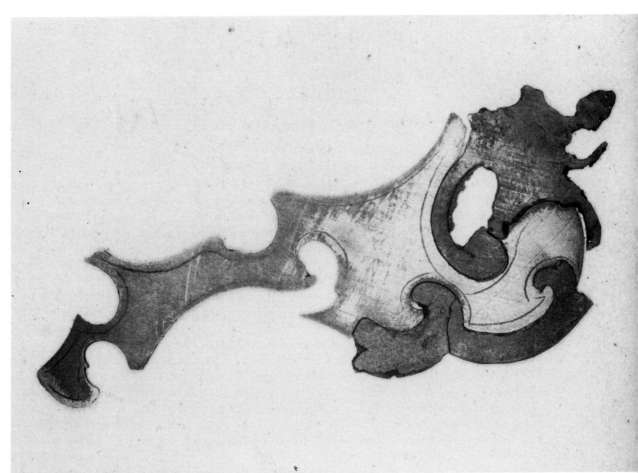

photo 169

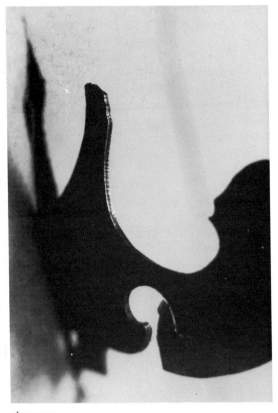

photo 170

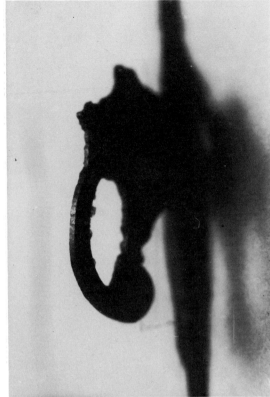

photo 171

manufacture no preparation of the back was undertaken. Using this method it would not be necessary, and this demonstrates well this method of pre-finishing before laying.

With photo 169 we are looking at a face surface; in the top-right sector where the shell joins the brass is an area looking like a comma. This area is very small, only 10mm ($\frac{3}{8}$ in) long, and just over 3 to 4mm ($\frac{5}{16}$ in) thick; the marks from the saw are clearly defined. The sawing is slow and not vertical, having been cut freehand by a saw-piercer (photo 170). Comparing this with photo 171, which shows the tiny piece of shell that has lain alongside it, we see that the sawing was quite different to that of the brass. It was fast, as would be expected for a much softer material. This shows us that template sawing was a common and much favoured practice with boullework.

Whichever way of making the surface has been used, whether the sandwich method or by cutting the metal first and using it for a template (as I prefer), eventually the work must be glued down. Many recipes for the glue have been recorded; all are recommended to verdigris the metal (to help adhesion) and to plasticize the glue; to ease the inevitable movement arising from the incompatibility of the materials. The recipes range from boiling garlic in the glue to using urine in it; they have all been tried! The results seem to be about the same – although I shall not be around to see if my glueing has survived for two or three hundred years! I do not know whether an analysis of glue from an original surface has ever been carried out; possibly I should have undertaken such a scheme myself. One thing is certain; it is always the metal that has the greater failure rate in a *boulle* surface, and (as stated earlier) the technique does require constant care and attention. Movement between the ground and surface will cause problems for any adhesive. I do not like to use modern chemical adhesives on an old *boulle* surface, preferring to keep the ability to reverse the process. I use a system taught to me many years ago by an old tradesman whose training began in the early 1880s. He recommended hot animal glue with some Venice turps added to it; this is the substance put on leather grips to make them tacky to the hand. A teaspoonful to a pint of glue was his recommendation – and it works. Whether it is satisfactory and will last I do not know; 25 to 30 years is not enough time to say.

If you do not require the work to be reversible, then modern adhesives can produce excellent results. I have a small pair of wine coolers that I veneered totally in copper; the groundwork is man-made stable laminboard and a modern two-part adhesive was used. The two materials appear totally compatible and nothing has moved. However, ten years is again not enough time to know for sure if the work's longevity will match that of a certain superb small table of *c.* 1680 veneered with pewter, brass and shell (colour plate (vii)). Histories and records of work always concentrate on the one- and two-part boulle. This table, which came through my workshop, was something very rare to see, since it was original. No restoration work was apparent at all, which is so rare as to be almost unknown. It carries a pair which belongs to Her Majesty the Queen, and is on loan to the Victoria & Albert Museum: one table is veneered with pewter and inlaid with brass and tortoiseshell, the other has a natural shell ground and is inlaid with pewter outfalls and brass.

Having a very intimate knowledge of the pewter table and having enjoyed a close scrutiny of the other, it is very hard to believe that the brass inlays on both tables would have been cut especially for the work, to create a pair. From the technique employed it must follow that a third surface would have been produced automatically if the template sawing method was used, which seems to be the case. If the design was first cut in the brass to produce the outfalls for the two existing tables, there would automatically be a brass ground veneer available. Using this as a template to cut the pewter ground would produce pewter outfalls to combine with the brass and inlay into the shell ground. Our first part-boulle would be a shell ground with brass dolphins and pewter fins – as in the table belonging to the Queen. The second cut, a pewter ground, would give a shell dolphin and brass fins as colour plate (viii). This is a totally practical and common-sense piece of reasoning from the workshop. The technique would involve a third-part cut of a brass ground with a pewter dolphin, with shell or coloured-horn fins. These can be deduced from the presence of two colours of shell within the two tables. When the pewter table came for restoration, had it been veneered with a brass ground with pewter and shell inlays, it would still have been completely accepted as the pair to the table from the Royal Collection.

For a tradesman this is a logical extension of an idea. The hardest material is the most difficult to work; in this case it is the brass. History accepts one- and two-part cutting, and by using the method of template sawing that seems to have been used on the Golle table, three-part can also be achieved.

— 7

Metal inlay: the technique

Commonly used metals are copper, tin, zinc and lead. Alloying them together will produce the materials for inlay and boullework.

Bronze an alloy of copper and tin.

Brass has a composition of roughly 70% copper and 30% zinc.

Dutch Metal 80% copper, 20% zinc, this carries a distinctly golden colour and is excellent for boullework (if obtainable).

Pewter an alloy of tin and lead, usually alloyed as 80% tin and 20% lead; the higher the lead content, the softer and duller the material, until a 50–50 proportion produces common solder.

Temperatures

These are important, and are worth trying to memorize. Copper has a melt-point of $1084°$ C, zinc is $419°$C. When alloyed together the resulting brass has a melt-point of about $680°$ C.

Lead melts at $326°$ C and tin at $232°$ C. Alloyed at 80% to 20%, the resulting pewter has a melt-point of $187°$ C.

Brass

These days brass sheet is rolled with total accuracy and then marketed at various thicknesses, known as gauges. 10 gauge is $\frac{1}{8}$ in; 12, 14, 16 follow. The higher the number the thinner the sheet, so 16 gauge is $\frac{1}{16}$ in; subsequent gauges are 18, 20, 22, and 24. Material for brass inlay and boullework comes within the last three. It is important when selecting your brass to note that it is sold as hard, half-hard and soft; it is best always to use the latter. The reason will become obvious when sawing begins; the vibration of the saw will be minimal working with soft brass.

The gauge chosen must be just a little thinner than the inlay material; it makes little difference if this inlay is a veneer; shell, horn, ivory or pearl. The reason has been given already; it will always be easier to bring the softer materials down to the harder brass than to bring brass down to the inlay level. Thought given to this will save much time and trouble when the work is finally laid. Naturally, if piercing or inlaying metals together, use the same gauge.

It has been found that for the repair of *boulle* from the seventeenth, eighteenth and early nineteenth century, 20 or 22 gauge metal is usually needed; work dating from after this time needs gauge 24. If new work is being carried out, 22 gauge should be your choice.

Use of soft brass is of vital importance, so the ways of annealing to create a soft and malleable metal should be familiar. Heat the metal on a fire brick surface to a uniform dull red, and allow it to cool naturally. Remember the melting point of the brass when small work is being softened.

Little else need be said before sawing can be attempted. It has been my experience that the most satisfactory way of sawing is by hand or with

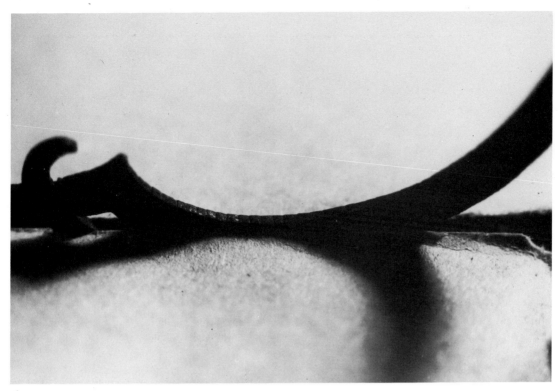

photo 172

a treadle fret. Any work is a time-consuming business and evidence of machinery is hard to find. Hand-operated band-saws show their use in boullework from about 1860 (photo 172). Other evidence always shows that sawing was by hand in the donkey or swing-saw. Modern jig-saws, with the necessary blades fitted, can be used. However, I have never mastered their use and prefer handwork, although this by no means rules them out. But with the intricacies of some work, hand-sawing is the only way. The control of the hand compared with a machine in these circumstances has to be experienced to be believed.

Assuming handwork is chosen, sawing frames designed for wood can be used, the only difference being in the saw blades. Saw blades have the prefix W for wood; with the metal-cutting or piercing-saws the prefix is M. Starting with M/o which is 10 in thick, .025 inch deep and with a tooth pitch of 60, we can reduce in size through M1/o, M2/o, M3/o to M4/o which is the finest, .006 in × .018 in with a tooth pitch of 80: this will saw material up to 20 gauge quite happily.

Similarly from Mo we can increase, M1, M2, M3, M4 to M5 the coarsest which is 0.17 in × .036 in, tooth pitch 32 – and will handle material to 10 gauge with ease. The blades I use are again Eclipse by Neill of Sheffield.

All cutting machinery depends upon its ability to remove the material being machined. The saw in your hand should be considered as a machine, and as with a machine, if too much material removal is attempted at one cut, failure of the saw will occur. To put it another way, use an M5 blade on 22 gauge metal and the results will be poor. Change the blade to an M4/o and the sawing will immediately become easier. As with wood, do not force the cut, and keep the saw as vertical as possible. Movement from the vertical to the left or right of the direction of cut will usually result in breakage of the blade. When sawing metal a minute quantity of lubricant on the saw blade will be helpful.

There are really no hard and fast rules for saw-piercing metal. At one time it was a trade in itself. Experience will very soon show you the direction

photo 173

photo 174

you need to follow. The best pointer I can give is to study the shape you want to cut and relate this to the gauge of metal being used. That is to say, if the work is small and tight in its design, the gauge must be kept to a minimum thickness. 20 gauge of .037 inch is the maximum that can normally be used. The feel of people's hands will always be different; there is really no substitute for experience, and no short-cut to acquiring skill.

When an intricate shape is to be sawn, render it down to the smallest area possible. Photo 173 shows an area to be sawn; the first cuts have rendered the work in half diagonally (photo 174). Smaller and smaller areas can now be sawn, the smaller the area the smaller the saw frame required, and the easier the work will become. One advantage with the piercing-saw is that one can adjust the tension of the saw blade, an important factor in the sawing of metal (photos 175, 176, 177, 178). Take your time during this operation, sawing metal is slow work when compared to wood.

Copper

This can be worked exactly as brass; the sawing is the same and can often be much easier. It will work-harden, as does brass, so it will need annealing. Unlike brass it can be quenched after heat-

ing; this is not necessary but can hurry up the proceedings.

Pewter

A lovely metal, it carries none of the properties of brass or copper. It does not need annealing, does not work-harden, is free-cutting and can be cut with a knife. The sawing and engraving is a pleasure. A metal with all these properties must have a drawback, and it does; a melt-point of 187°C. My ignorance of this was revealed by using too much heat in the laying of a lifted surface. It can be likened to dealing with solder; the low melt-point must always be kept in mind.

Pewter rot has been mentioned and will often be seen as a loss of metal at the edge of a saw cut. Blisters appear and become holes. Fillers are a useful addition to the repairer, metallic sealing wax is worth experiment (beeswax and rosin in a proportion of 3–1 melted with pewter). Brass or copper dust added can also make useful fillers. With pewter we are lucky to have a material called Woods metal, an alloy of bismuth, lead, tin and cadmium in a proportion of 4, 2, 1, 1. This has a melt-point of 71°C and because of this is an ideal material for stopping or as filler in the repair of pewter. Pewter can be difficult to obtain in small quantities; thought should be given to the use of

photo 175

photo 176

photo 177

photo 178

aluminium, which can be a good match in colour and a useful way of getting over the problem. The cutting properties of aluminium are a cross between pewter and brass, and it does not require annealing.

Laying of a surface

The surface when put together will follow the methods of wood marquetry; the difference is only in the materials used.

The most important thing is that the underside of the metal at the glueing surface is clean, and *well* toothed or scratched. If the surface is *boulle*, only the metal is treated in this way. When the surface is a metal inlaid into a veneer, go over the whole undersurface again, bringing the wood into the toothing pattern. Treat it as if the whole surface were wood. The process from here is exactly as for wood; the press is the same and if hot glue is used, this procedure is exactly the same as well. The only addition would be a sheet of 16 gauge metal, ideally copper, used as the heat source for the caul. Even this is not necessary; hardboard or masonite can be substituted.

The temperature used is important; the normal workshop method is crude but effective. If spittle bounces straight off the metal of the caul it is too hot, but if it stays and boils the heat is correct. If hardboard or masonite is used, heat it until too hot for the hand to touch.

The adhesives are many and varied, and I must again emphasize the importance of the ability to reverse the glue process. If this is not considered necessary, the Evodes can be effective. Epoxy resins, used with thought and care, are also excellent, though the adhesive and the materials being used are often going to be very foreign to each other. To lay a complete and newly-cut boullework or brass inlaid surface, hot animal glue is the answer, but when repair is undertaken, the alternatives will come into their own.

Repair

Before any repair is undertaken, it must be fully understood that there are no satisfactory short cuts. Any repair work will be tedious, often requiring great patience. A bad *boulle* or brass inlay repair will usually take just as long as a good one. All work will be time-consuming, and therefore expensive.

The most common problem with these surfaces will be metal loss. The impracticality of glueing metal to wood is the usual reason. Dampness causes the glue to swell and this pushes the metal out of place. However, one cause of metal loss and lifting is quite simply cleaning, and this is one very good reason for a plate-glass cover for a metal inlaid top.

Time and again when repair is asked to be undertaken on a bent and mangled piece of brass or pewter inlay, which has been saved to be replaced, it would usually be far easier to re-cut and replace the loss; more often I am asked to replace these pieces and it can be difficult in the extreme. Photo 179 is an example of brass from a late-nineteenth-century table. The method of straightening this out for replacement is gently to take out the worst kinks and bends with snipe-nose pliers. Even this amount of movement can harden the brass, so anneal, and be very cautious. The sizes of brass vary, as the illustration shows. Some areas will heat far quicker than others. Watch this carefully; with very small and thin parts melting can occur, so be gentle.

When annealed, lay the brass face-down on a smooth metal surface and gently blanish the back with a small, light hammer. Emphasis is laid on the word gentle; it is very easy to work-harden the brass, and make further annealing necessary. With patience the piece can be straightened and photo 180 shows the back ready for replacement. This piece of brass was sawn in 1870, and photo 172 shows its sawing, carried out by a hand-operated bandsaw in common use at that time.

Photo 181 is a piece of damaged pewter. This does not need annealing. The straightening is very simple and the flat part of a hammer or veneering hammer run over the back will take out all but the worst dents; which can be removed by gentle blanishing, as for brass. This illustration also shows the toothing of the metal, vital for the good glueing of metal to wood. Photos 120 and 121 of the bracket show another common prob-

photo 179

photo 180

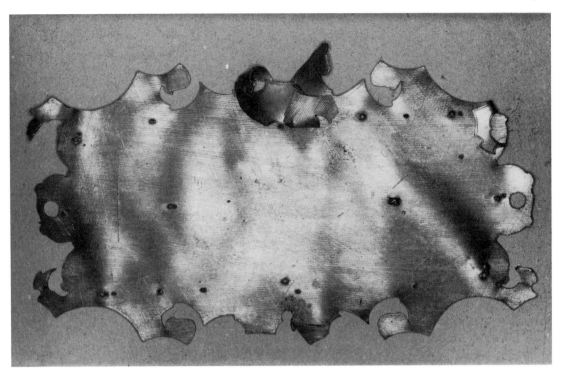

photo 181

lem and cause of damage; the practice of crudely nailing down the surface. The way to repair this is to rivet a plug into place, flush the surfaces off and re-lay (diagram 52). Strangely, this practice of nailing down is a common one and was used from the beginning; it can be a most advantageous method of holding awkward areas if done correctly. The old way, as used in the production of boullework, was to make a small square tapered brass pin (or with pewter a pin made from tin). Driving into place rivetted the head over, and this was flushed down to the surface, and if necessary engraved over.

This is without doubt the best way but it is expensive. A simpler and much cheaper way is to use a brass gimp pin; their diameter is .036 in or 36 thousand parts of an inch. A 1MM or no. 59 drill is .037 in and makes an ideal combination with the brass gimp. The method is simple. Drill the metal, cut the head off the gimp, put adhesive as necessary into place, then push the brass into position and gently drive the pin down. The act of hammering will mushroom the pin into a tiny

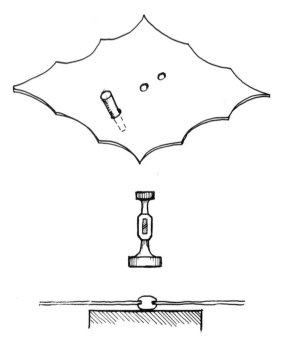

diagram 52

rivet head. When the glues have dried completely it can then be flushed down and if necessary engraved over.

One problem that will be encountered is small lifts and loose pieces; the household duster being the usual culprit. Clean any old glue from under the lifted or loose piece. The choice of repair glue is wide. Evostik, the many epoxy resins, and numerous brands with the capability of glueing metal, ceramics and wood are available. The choice can be yours, but I do not advise using the super-glues with their added capability of glueing you together! *Before any glueing is started, make sure you have the means to put the repair under pressure while the glue sets.*

When all this has been arranged, put the adhesive in place and push the metal into position. Wipe away surplus glue, cover the area with thin polythene and put the area under pressure until the glue has set. These glues are irreversible; after wiping off the surplus glue put a thin film of furniture or wax polish is put over the surface (before the polythene); any glue that does find its way on to the surface will not stick.

The old method with brass was to prepare the lift as above, but instead of glue some powdered flake shellac was used. A hot iron, such as a small soldering iron, was used to melt this when the brass was pushed back into place. When the iron was taken away, the brass was held until it cooled and the lift would usually stay down. *Do not* attempt this with pewter.

The usual repairs to the surfaces will include replacement of loss. Copies of small areas can be taken by rubbing, tracing or drawing. With a brass-inlaid wood surface, the process of making the repair slightly oversize, and then using the knife to cut it into place, can be used. More often than not the replacement will have to be put into a metal, shell, or other surface that cannot be successfully cut with a knife. The only method then is to cut accurately and make a final fitting with files before the repair can be put in place.

Before any replacement can be carried out, all the old adhesive must be removed. Usually you will be faced with animal glue. Dampness is usually the problem; this causes the glue to swell, and since the materials are not absorbent they

have only one way to go, upward, and so lift and come off. The only way is to remove the glue. This is tedious, and involves the scraping away of the dead and dry glue from the area of loss. A tip: when a replacement is going into place, should the metal be thicker than the original, remove some of the wood ground to allow the replacement to lie flush with the surface. It will be difficult if the metal surface has to be flushed down.

The usual problem with brass lines and decorative bands is shrinkage across the grain. Lifts and buckles will be commonplace. Assuming the wood will not shrink any more, lift the brass line and shorten it at the mitre (diagram 53). Similarly, if a band shows a buckle, slip a brass shim under the lift, saw it through with a jeweller's saw, lay one side and reduce the other until it lies flat. Usually the saw-cut will remove a sufficiency of metal; it is, however, a good idea to leave a slight gap to allow for further shrinkage, should it occur (diagram 54).

When dealing with brass lines, use of the scratchstock will be helpful (diagram 55). The brass line is a very common form of inlay, and lines of $\frac{1}{16}$ in, $\frac{1}{8}$ in square and their metric equivalents are readily available. Make up your scratch out of 16 gauge plate or silver-steel sheet; a small cabinet scraper is ideal. File up the scratch as diagram 55a, so that the tooth is fractionally smaller than the metal line. When the groove in

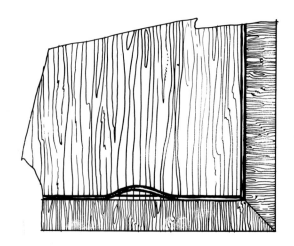

diagram 53

the surface has been scratched out, the metal should be a *tight* push fit into the groove. Time spent on achieving this will pay dividends, since the brass can now be laid without adhesive or using a minimal amount. Always if possible use square material; curves will be far easier to follow. Anneal the metal, if brass; place it in a piece of steel tube and heat the tube. This is vital since it

will stop the metal kinking, and therefore make the laying far easier. Laid with care, paying attention to the groove depth; it is possible to lay brass lines so that no flushing down to the surface will be necessary.

This piece of equipment was used extensively for the production of mouldings – the necessary shapes being filed into metal, as the diagram shows. This very simple gadget has many uses and will shape ivory, tortoiseshell, and even brass when an initial rough shape has been made.

To make a complete *boulle* or brass-inlaid piece of furniture would not be within the ambitions of most people! The method is time-consuming and needs planning. The first consideration is the design. Since the system will produce a one- and two-part cut, the planning must take this into account, even if the outfalls are not to be used. Suppose the top is 1 metre (39 in) by 600mm (24 in) and is to be of brass inlaid with shell. The first need is a sheet of soft 22 gauge brass to these dimensions. Study the design so that the sheet can be rendered down to small areas. If the design is traditional it will be found that this can be achieved so that the one- and two-part cut is maintained. In fact this tends to be built-in to traditional designs, so that areas 250mm(10 in) by 200mm (8 in) are commonplace. If the design is your own, set it up so that this is possible.

The first stage is to tooth up the glueing side of the brass, making certain that the whole surface is well covered. The next stage is to put the design on the brass. How this is done is up to you. Engrave it, or glue a photocopy on to the surface.

Sawing can now begin. As each piece is sawn out, lay it on another pattern. When the section is fully cut, re-assemble it on the pattern; this will be a time-consuming and tedious job. When all the pieces are cut, the inlays for a brass ground can be made up. If using coloured horn, prepare what is necessary and use the system of template sawing to put the pieces into place, making sure that they are slightly thicker than the metal used.

Hold each piece in place; masking tape or a glued paper is ideal for this job. Thought must be given to the fact that in rendering the sheet to manageable sizes, there will be many inlays where this has taken place; two sawings will be necessary

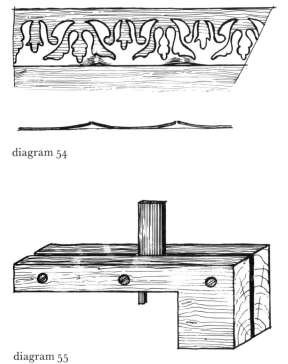

diagram 54

diagram 55

diagram 55a

in consequence. Where these are situated can be seen when the sawn sheet is placed on the assembly pattern.

The easiest way to glue the inlay to the brass for template sawing is as follows: cover the inlay horn with masking tape and use Evode contact adhesive to fix this to the brass. When sawn, the tape can be peeled from the inlay and will come away easily from the metal. Any adhesive left can be easily removed with a proprietary cleaner.

This method is excellent for any template sawing; it will also protect wood surfaces from the possible staining caused by these adhesives. When the top is completed, it needs to be held together. Masking tape can be more convenient than the usual practice of glueing paper. When laying is finished; the tape removed, the inlaid areas flushed down to the metal and the surface burnished; then the important process of engraving can begin.

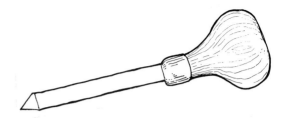

diagram 56

Engraving

This makes or breaks the end result. Surfaces will often be seen where most of the engraving has worn away; this is not a natural process but is caused by poor repair. The repairers sometimes lack the skills to replace engraving, but a far more frequent cause is that an article repaired years ago was just not worth the expense of having the engraving re-furbished.

For the person who wants seriously to achieve success, engraving is a must. Either the skills of an engraver must be purchased, or these skills obtained by practice. When a small area needs to be copied or picked up, it is well worth trying your hand.

The necessary tools can be purchased, or a small Swiss pattern file adapted (diagram 56). Make sure the handle is comfortable when gripped in your palm; the index finger rests on the flat part of the triangle and guides the cut. I recommend the Swiss pattern because a variety can be purchased with an inbuilt flexibility, so the breakages associated with these can be eliminated. Grind the cutting surfaces off the file, then shape and grind the cutting edge as the diagram shows. These tiny malleable files are

invaluable when flushing the heads of fixing pins; they can instantly become custom-shaped riflers ideal for the job.

Sharpen the cutting face with a stone. The lower point of the triangle in the diagram becomes your engraving point. Practise on a waste piece of metal; you will soon feel when you are cutting correctly. Never use too much pressure; the angle of cut will soon be apparent. Always draw a line and follow that; never practise with random cuts. Always draw the work you want, never try to cut freehand. Be gentle and you will be surprised at what can be achieved.

If major metal replacement has taken place it will have been an expensive undertaking. If engraving is necessary, and the necessary skills are not to hand, the work should be put into the care of a skilled person.

Cleaning and Polishing

On brass-inlaid and boullework surfaces one material is taboo: *metal polish*. It will darken wooden ground and can cause severe and irremovable staining. Since we are going to be presented with a surface that can carry a diverse selection of materials, a universal way of cleaning is required. Unfortunately, the metals will often carry verdigris to a greater or lesser extent. When severe it can be pushed off with a brass scraper, although this is very much a last resort. The problem is rarely encountered, and will usually apply only to a surface untouched since its manufacture.

The problem can be solved by mild abrasion. The finest grade wet and dry emery paper, if used gently with some salt or lemon juice in the water, gives excellent results. Never get anything wet; allow the verdigris that comes off to become a paste but no damper.

Both of these situations are rare. The usual surface will show evidence of polish, which can be seen as lighter or less-tarnished areas. This must be removed using oooo steel wool and alcohol. Steel wool must be used with care or more pieces of metal could be hooked or pulled up. When the polish has been removed, cleaning the surface can be tackled. With a brass inlay into wood, a 30% solution of oxalic acid used over the metal will produce almost instant results. Have plenty of ventilation, use rubber gloves and do not use steel wool. A coarse cheesecloth with a little rotten stone or rouge powder moistened with the acid solution will be all that is necessary.

Oxalic acid comes in a crystal form and is soluble in warm water. It is a distillation from the green leaves of rhubarb and is a bad irritant; use it with care. After use, wipe over the work with vinegar or a solution of bicarbonate of soda. Again I stress rubber gloves; a barrier cream is not sufficient.

The same process can be used successfully over a boullework surface, remembering to wipe over with the vinegar, etc. During cleaning it is possible that the enhancing of the engraving could become loose; put this back with the traditional heelball if available. If not, a black wax crayon can be satisfactory. (Heelball consists of beeswax, rosin and soot).

The polishing of these surfaces is always a problem. With a brass-inlaid surface one can be heavy-handed when cutting-down, to stop a build-up of polish over the metal. Since the metal will always stand a little proud of the surface (a fortunate perk of veneering a hard and soft material together, caused by the greater glue shrinkage of the wood) stopping this polish build-up will not be difficult. In the final stage a good work-over with a well-thinned polish will produce a good finish on the metal, without the blooming and discolouration often associated with finishes on these surfaces.

A boullework surface must be approached using a minimum of polish. The recommended polish is a transparent shellac, of the best quality available. My own method is to thin the polish severely, breaking it down to one-third polish and two-thirds alcohol. Use a lubricant on the rubber from the beginning – white oil or a raw linseed. The trick is not to use an over-full rubber; a half-full rubber is best. Use more oil on the rubber than usual. You can mix oil with the polish and alcohol, but this needs experience. Use a lot of pressure; this will be necessary, since the rubber is not full. Work slowly over the surface: care must be taken with the direction of the work to avoid pulling up fine points in the design. A boullework surface will respond very quickly to this form of polishing. When fully dry, the usual practice of spiriting out to remove the oil is an easy process. Remember the surface is not absorbent; polish will remain lying on the surface to a far greater degree than with wood. Ideally, a surface when polished should appear just burnished, as if there were no varnish on it at all.

Copying

Photo 182 is a brass inlay surface of brass and ebony before repair. My method of copying for repairs is shown in photo 183. A photograph of photo 182 has been taken, and enlarged to exactly the size of the work. In photo 183 the negative has been reversed and printed: the join of the two prints can be seen. The result is a picture of the surface fully repaired. The necessary repair area can now be sawn from the photograph. This allows the character of work to be copied, something not always possible from a drawing or tracing. It is an ideal method, since once a photographic print is available, as many copies as necessary can be run off cheaply by photocopying. And, when a complicated surface has to be repaired, a photograph will pick up the more minute detail often lost with a rubbing, tracing or drawing.

The brass inlay of photo 184 is of stamped brass and the area of loss can be seen by the rosewood veneer. A rubbing has been taken from the other side of the table and the result is photo 185. Two small areas of Greek key were also missing; these pieces can take four hours to cut, as already discussed in Chapter 5. Photo 186 shows the

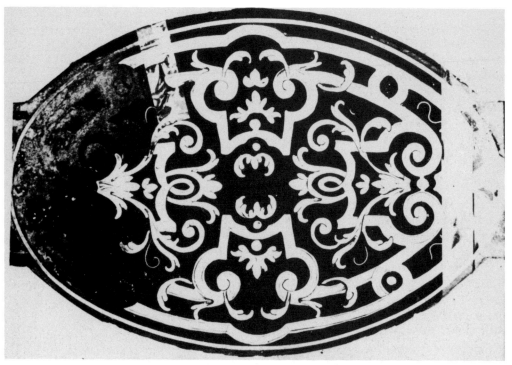

photo 182

photo 183

photo 184

photo 185

photo 186

initial sawing in brass. Template sawing around the metal was the method used, and the tightness of the resultant join can be seen in photo 187. The frailty of the hand when compared with mechanical work is very apparent. The last illustration of the sequence, photo 188, shows the undamaged side of the table.

Photos 189 and 190 again show template sawing. In this case, as with the key, individual start-holes are necessary and can always be seen. The sawing of an inlay for a rosewood ground is shown in photo 191. The result, when in place, shows the accuracy of jointwork and how clearly the shape can be followed (photo 192).

The cutting of tortoiseshell is achieved in the same way. It will hold up well to a very fine cut, as photos 193 and 194 show. The final illustration, photo 195, shows a piece of shell after sawing. The speed of cutting can be seen, and is at least twice the speed of metal; and as with wood, the speed of cut has to be controlled carefully. Photo 196 is the

end result. This brass is from the early eighteenth century; the shell and template sawing are modern. Again, the difference in the sawing is very apparent.

Tortoiseshell and Horn

To show the difference between the Greenback turtle and the Hawksbill is difficult. Photo 197 is the Greenback, which carries the rather elongated mottles. Photo 198 is the Hawksbill, which carries a rather random mottle. In the best examples this becomes very pale and produces the finest shell to interpret the glue undercolours.

The preparation needs no further explanation, but the method of achieving the required colour does. The ingredients are the shell or horn, the best quality vellum paper, a supply of water-solvent poster paints in powder form, and animal glue or PVA. If PVA is used, experiment with the powder colours. You may find the glue thickens

photo 187

photo 188

photo 189

photo 190

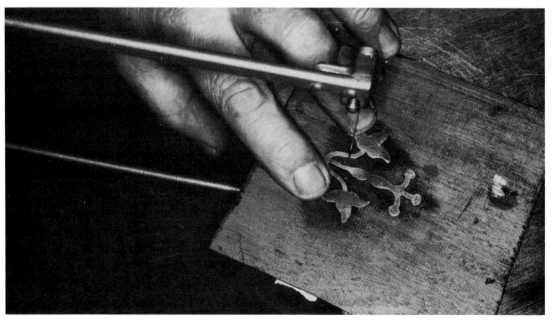

photo 191

up too much and dilution is necessary; test glueings are a must.

The powder colours can be whatever you wish. If copying an existing colour, experiments on the shell will soon show the mix required. When this is found and hot animal glue is being used, dilute it by about 15%, and mix up a sufficiency of colour with the glue. Apply this to the vellum paper and the shell or horn; put the surfaces together and place in a simple press, as made up for laying a surface. With animal glue use a *little* heat, and do not use too much pressure. A good proportion of the glue needs to be left between the paper and shell or bare patches will result. Experiment will show the way, and this is yet another reason to use an adhesive that is easily reversible. When the scute or horn has been prepared, always keep it under pressure. The easiest way is between two pieces of chipboard under weights, or with clamps which will prevent the glue from pulling.

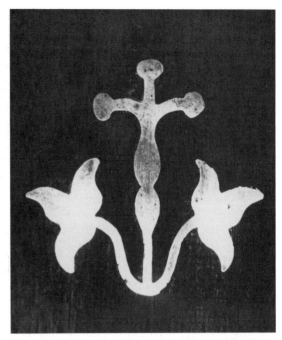

photo 192

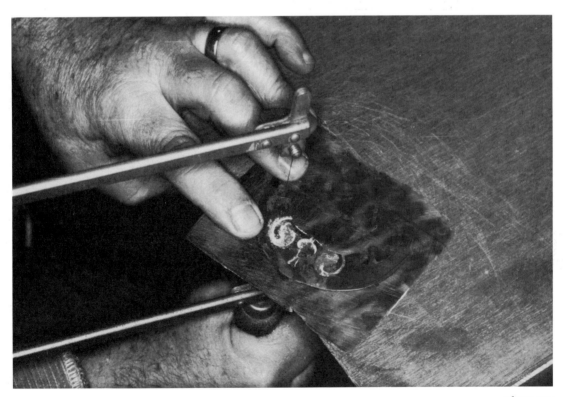

photo 193

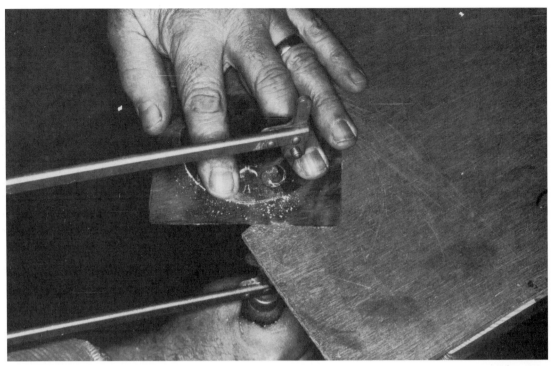

photo 194

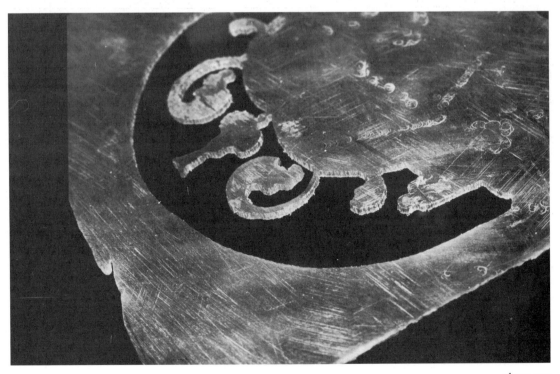

photo 195

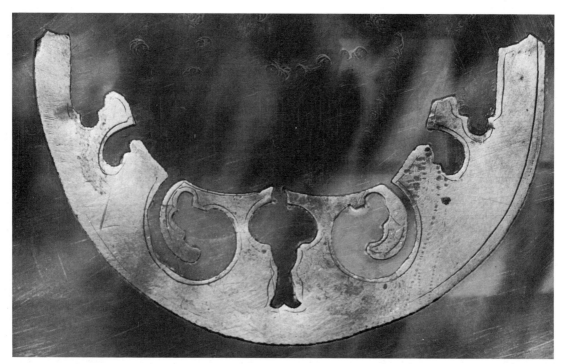

photo 196

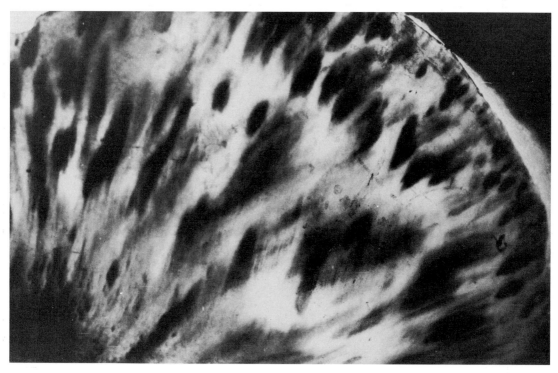

photo 197

Finally, we come to the use of substitutes. Celluloid was a favourite in the late nineteenth century. Always a bright red colour, it can usually be recognized by the fact that it does not lift or lip round the edges, but from the centre – almost as a bubble. A sure test is to lay it with heat; shell and horn will stand as much if not more heat than wood, while the substitutes will shrivel. To lay these blisters, the best way is to pierce them with a needle in a drill. Thin glue can be rubbed through the holes and pressure applied. Be cautious about using heat; it may be best not to use it at all.

Horn substitutes can be difficult: the best is probably acetate sheet. Given a fine abrasion on the back it is compatible with coloured animal glues and PVA. Epoxy resins if thinned enough can be coloured and used for small areas. Another method when synthetics are used is to colour the ground first: when everything is dry the sheet can be glued into place. The obvious advantage here is that materials that are totally compatible with each other can be selected and used – a luxury not always possible when the older techniques are employed.

Ivory

Raw ivory is expensive and difficult to obtain. When new it is very white and soft, and the colour of the ground will usually show through. Colouring of the adhesive with zinc or flake white powder is advised.

Usually repair will be carried out with pieces of old ivory. The sources are many; trophies, souvenirs from the East, billiard balls and the most common, piano keys. The sawing is a pleasure. Use the finest of piercing saws and no problems will be presented. Saw it as you would saw brass. Ivory is compatible with all adhesives, and if old ivory is used it will often not be necessary to colour it. Nevertheless, the habit of whitening the adhesive is a good one.

The cleaning of ivory should be undertaken with care: I recommend surgical spirit used sparingly. Do not use any abrasives at all. If engraving is necessary, treat the material as if it were brass with a grain running in it. The grain of ivory, like the grain of wood, is important. Before

photo 198

working with the material, look it over carefully. The grain will soon be seen; always work with it in mind.

Loose pieces of ivory are best lifted and cleaned before re-laying. The grain will often cause curling and warping. This can be difficult to straighten; the safest and simplest way is to soak in hot water. Do *not* boil. Place the ivory between *white* paper and put it under pressure. This will usually be effective, but a persistent lift may need further treatment. Fasten it down with a fine tapered pin fashioned from ivory, or a matching plastic.

The substitute for ivory is celluloid, which is very prevalent as stringwork and small stylized flowers in furniture *c.*1890–1910. Always be cautious if the presence of this is suspected; use no heat or acetone based glues. *Ivorine* is the name for modern inlay lines or sheets used as a substitute.

Pearl

This is a most awkward material; very hard and slow cutting. Photos 199 and 200 show the problems involved. The brittleness is very evident and even a tiny piece such as this has been template-sawn. The supply is also difficult; pearl

photo 199

photo 200

photo 201

buttons are almost a thing of the past, and their makers were usually the source of supply for pearl veneers.

Raw shells will produce the pearl if you are prepared to grind them down. The ear shell will provide pearl often up to 20mm ($\frac{3}{4}$ in) thickness. The abalone provides almost every colour imaginable. Synthetics are made which will give a very passable imitation of pearl and can often be used satisfactorily.

When sawing pearl, use a sawing platform with a sawcut instead of a V (diagram 41); it will need far more support around the sawing area than any other material. Large pieces of pearl are not obtainable and never have been. Large areas will have to be put together in a regular pattern and become part of the design or assembled as in photo 201.

This monogram has been put together almost as crazy paving glued on to paper. A white-coloured glue has been used; when dry, the shape is cut out and sawn into the shell. The problems of engraving can clearly be seen. The material has a tendency to flake and crack, a snag you will encounter when sawing.

Engraving can also be carried out by etching with acid. The process is the usual one of a wax covering, the pattern then cut in the wax so that the pearl is exposed, and acid then used to etch the exposed surface. This method is described in some books, but I would not recommend it myself.

Pearl with no polish on it can be cleaned simply with soap, or a mild detergent and water. One traditional method that works very well is warm tea, and this will also help to enhance the iridescence. A polish such as shellac can be removed only with alcohol, and strippers or caustics are not to be recommended. Finally, when cutting pearl, always select the finest piercing or jeweller's saw you can.

Bibliography

Bradley, Ian, *A History of Machine Tools*, M.A.P. Publications Ltd

The Cabinet-Makers London Book of Prices 1793 (reprint), *The Journal of The Furniture History Society*, Victoria & Albert Museum, 1983

Cescinsky, Herbert, *The Gentle Art of Faking Furniture*, Dover Publications Inc, New York

Diderot & d'Alemberts Encyclopédie volume IV, 1765

Fine Woodworking Magazine, no 27, The Taunton Press Inc, Newtown, Connecticut, USA, March–April 1981

Gilbert, Christopher, *The Life & Work of Thomas Chippendale*, Studio Vista, Christies, London

Hayward, Helena, *World Furniture*, Paul Hamlyn, 1965

Household Furniture & Interior Decoration Executed from Designs by Thomas Hope, Longman, Hurst, Rees and Orme, London, 1807

Lambert, Deborah, 'The Rescue of the Petworth Panels', *Christies International Magazine*, September–October 1984

de Montebello, Philippe, 'Notable Acquisitions 1983–1984', *The Metropolitan Museum of Art*, The Metropolitan Museum of Art

Roubo, Jacob Andre, *L'Art de l'Ebenisterie, L'Arte du Menuserie*, 1770

Scientific American volume 3 no 37, New York, 1848

Styles, Libraire Larousse, Middle Ages – Louis XV, 1972

Thornton, Peter, 'The Furnishings & Decoration of Ham House', *Furniture History*, Furniture History Society and Victoria & Albert Museum, 1980

Wilson, Gillian, *The Decorative Arts in the J. Paul Getty Museum* (selections from), Bookstore, J. Paul Getty Museum, California, USA

Watson, Sir Francis, *The Wrightsman Collection*, volumes I & II, The Metropolitan Museum of Art, New York Graphic Society, Greenwich, Connecticut, USA

Suppliers

F. Friedlein & Co Ltd
6–10 Tring Close
Newbury Park
Ilford
Essex 1G2 7LJ
— Ivory, shells etc.

North Heigham Sawmills
Paddock Street
Norwich
Norfolk NR2 4TW
— Exotic hardwoods, veneer

David Russell Young
7134 Balboa Boulevard
Van Nuys
California 91406
U.S.A.
— Pearl, abalone blanks

J. Crispin & Sons
92/96 Curtain Road
Shoreditch
London EC2 A3AA
— Veneer, inlays

James Neill Tools
James Neill (Sheffield) Ltd
Sheffield
— Eclipse saws, also from any good tool merchant

Les Fils de J. George
96 à 100 Avenue Galliéni
93170 Bagnolet
Paris
— Veneer and hardwoods

Clay Bros
Metal Supplies Ltd
24 The Green
High Street
Ealing
London W5 5DA
— Small metal supplies, sheet and strip

Cayman Turtle Farm Ltd
PO Box 645
Grand Cayman
Cayman Islands
— Green turtle shell. Import licence required

W. S. Jenkins & Co. Ltd
Jeco Works
Tariff Road
Tottenham
London N17 0EN
— Polish and colour merchants

Halesowen Horn Co.
Halesowen
Near Birmingham
— Raw horn, also small cleared horn

Index